1994

The Synagogues and Churches
of Ancient Palestine

Leslie J. Hoppe, O.F.M.

A Michael Glazier Book
THE LITURGICAL PRESS
Collegeville, Minnesota

A Michael Glazier Book published by The Liturgical Press

Cover: Synagogue of Capernaum. Photo and design by Robin Pierzina, O.S.B.

1	2	3	4	5	6	7	8	9

Library of Congress Cataloging-in-Publication Data

Hoppe, Leslie J.
   The synagogues and churches of ancient Palestine / Leslie J.
Hoppe.
     p.   cm.
   "A Michael Glazier book."
   Includes bibliographical references.
   ISBN 0-8146-5754-0
   1. Synagogue architecture—Palestine. 2. Church architecture-
-Palestine. 3. Architecture, Byzantine—Palestine.
   4. Architecture, Ancient—Palestine. 5. Basilicas—Influence.
   I. Title.
NA5977.H66 1994
726'.3'0933—dc20   93-28695
                                      CIP

Contents

Introduction

The Jews and the Christians who lived in Palestine during the first seven centuries of the Common Era have left to those who have come after them a great amount of information about their religious beliefs. Believing Jews and Christians today look back at this formative period in their respective traditions and consider the religious beliefs and practices of their predecessors as normative to some extent. Jews look to the Mishnah and the Talmud as sources of these normative affirmations and negations, while Christians look to the New Testament, the decisions of the first Ecumenical Councils and, to some extent, the writings of the Church Fathers for guidance in shaping their response to Jesus' proclamation of the reign of God. Both Christians and Jews look to the *literary* legacy of their traditions for information about the way their ancestors believed and lived. To the extent that they rely solely on literary works, they deprive themselves of a surprising amount of what the people of antiquity left for those who were to come after them. Our ancestors have left behind an enormous quantity of *nonliterary* sources that reveal much about what our ancestors believed and how they lived. Literary sources, after all, were produced by an elite class of believers and therefore do not always clearly reflect popular culture and religion.

Archaeology is the science that brings to light the material remains that the people of antiquity have left behind; and more importantly, archaeology offers an interpretation of these remains so that we can learn what they reveal about the culture of the people who produced and used them. At one time archaeology was concerned only with unearthing and describing artifacts and architecture in order to suggest the history of a site's occupation. Today, archaeology provides much more. It is helping us to understand something of the daily life, religion, economy, and politics of the people of Palestine in the Roman and Byzantine eras. Sometimes, the picture archaeology paints can help correct what may be a less-than-objective view presented in the literary material.

Both Jewish and Christian texts, for example, describe the growing gulf between Christianity and Judaism that took place in the Roman and Byzantine eras. These texts form the first chapter of a long and tragic history between these two faiths which have so much in common, for each, in its own way, is an heir to the religion of ancient Israel. Yet, excavation of some Roman-Byzantine sites in Palestine has shown that relations between Jews and Christians were not acrimonious, and may perhaps have even been cordial. Capernaum, a city with strong ties to the traditions about Jesus' Galilean ministry, became a center of Christian pilgrimage because one house there was venerated as that of Simon Peter's where Jesus found hospitality (see Mark 1:29-31). Despite the strong Christian presence in that city and the anti-Jewish legislation of the Byzantine emperors, the Jews of Capernaum built a strikingly beautiful synagogue just a few feet from the Christian sanctuary built by Christians in honor of Peter. Evidently, the Jews and the Christians of Capernaum learned how to live together in peace. Preliminary excavations of Sepphoris show that the town's population—made up of Christians, Jews, and adherents of Roman religions—managed to live together in harmony. Sepphoris was the capital of Lower Galilee. It was where Judah the Prince compiled the Mishnah. Its bishop attended the Council of Nicaea. The legacy left by the people of Capernaum and Sepphoris should lead believers to forswear the mistrust and polemics that still characterize some interchanges between Jews and Christians today.

Many early Christian texts are guilty of caricaturing Judaism, and early Jewish texts are just as guilty of caricaturing Christianity. An analysis of material remains unearthed by archaeology offers the possibility of painting a much more realistic portrait of early Judaism and Christianity. Archaeology shows what a diverse and creative phenomenon each religious tradition was. It allows people today from each tradition to understand the origins of the other without receiving the false impressions that sometimes come from reading literary texts alone.

This book deals with one way both early Jews and Christians expressed their religious beliefs: through the construction of places of worship. The synagogue and the church are not simply buildings; they are testimonies of faith. They do not simply shelter worshippers from the elements; they provide worshippers with a tangible way to express their beliefs. They are not erected haphazardly; they are built with care and a sensitivity that reveals the convictions of their builders. Study of the early synagogues and churches is one way to begin understanding and appreciating the *total* legacy that our ancestors in faith left for us.

An appreciation of early Jewish and Christian religious architecture is not the *sole* way to overcome our overdependence upon literary sources, but it is one place to begin. More data have to be gathered and interpreted before a complete picture of early Judaism and Christianity can emerge. In recent years archaeologists have become more aware of their responsibility to do more than describe their findings; they know that they also are responsible for *interpreting* the results of their excavations so as to reconstruct, as far as possible, the world in which our ancestors lived. This book does not pretend to accomplish that, since it is narrowly focused on just one feature of that world. What it is concerned to show is that archaeology does more than display interesting but ultimately irrelevant data. Archaeology can provide us with a new way of understanding the most important elements of our religious traditions.

Hundreds of ancient synagogues and churches have been excavated in Palestine. Sometimes the excavations have been thorough and careful; at other times they have been severely deficient. In any case, a book such as this one cannot provide a comprehensive picture of the achievements in the archaeology of Roman and Byzantine Palestine. Instead, specific sites and their structures have been chosen to give the reader a hint of how archaeology has contributed to an understanding of early Judaism and Christianity. Sites were chosen because they illustrate the variety of architectural styles in diverse areas throughout the entire period under study. Another criterion for selection has been the accessibility of these sites. Most of the synagogues and churches discussed in the book can be visited in Israel today. Occupation of a site after the Byzantine period, similarly, does not receive much attention. Though the Crusaders built many churches in Palestine, their work is not the concern of this book.

Several of the churches that are considered are still in use because they continue to attract Christian pilgrims. Others have been incorporated into archaeological parks by the Israeli Department of Antiquities. None of the ancient synagogues are in use today, though the Department of Antiquities requires that archaeologists attempt to restore ancient sites as they are being excavated.[1] After one particular ancient synagogue was excavated and restored, a ceremony of rededi-

---

[1] Archaeologists have to contend with the religious sensibilities of people who sometimes object to the excavation of religious sites. For a comment by one archaeologist on these problems, see Eric M. Meyers, "The Current State of Galilean Synagogue Studies," *The Synagogue in Late Antiquity*, Lee I. Levine (Philadelphia: The American Schools of Oriental Research, 1987) 126–27.

cation was held. It was a poignant attempt to reach back through the ages. That is just what archaeology tries to do. It tries to help us cross the gulf created by history so that we can converse with, and learn from, our ancestors in the faith.

Chapter 1

The Synagogue: Preliminary Issues

Introduction

Excavations in Palestine have uncovered thirty-six structures clearly identified as synagogues. The location of another forty-eight structures, from which architectural fragments have survived, is unknown. Finally, there are about sixty buildings whose identification as synagogues is in some dispute (see illust. 1).[1] In a book such as this, selections need to be made regarding which synagogues to treat since only a few can be treated at some length. My selections have been made in order to present synagogues from each of the three categories given above, to highlight a few important structures, and to give some idea of the architectural and artistic diversity that existed in synagogues of antiquity.

This chapter deals with the origin, function, and architectural form of synagogues. The next chapter deals with two very important synagogues from Galilee. The Galilean synagogue at Capernaum has long attracted attention. At first, this was because of its supposed connection with Jesus. Later, the beauty of the building itself captured the imagination of archaeologists, historians of art, and historians of religion. More recently this synagogue has been at the center of a controversy among archaeologists because of a dispute regarding its date. Another Galilean synagogue that merits attention is the one at Nabratein. What is unique about this ancient building is that it has yielded the only Torah shrine to be recovered in Palestine.

The third chapter deals with the synagogues of Judea. Though the center of early Judaism shifted from Judea to Galilee after the unsuccessful revolts against Roman rule, this region has yielded some significant synagogues, two of which served the needs of Samaritans. The fourth chapter presents four synagogues whose ornamentation is, at first, somewhat of a problem: the floors of the synagogues were adorned with a zodiac depicting a Greek god as the centerpiece. Ex-

---

[1] These numbers will increase when surveys of Golan are completed.

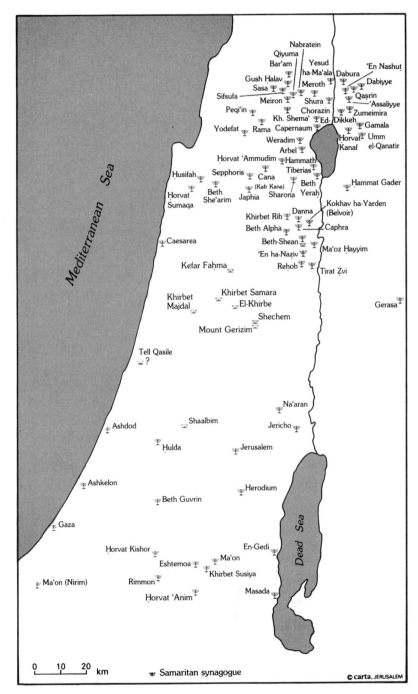

ILLUSTRATION 1. MAP OF ANCIENT SYNAGOGUE SITES IN PALESTINE. Note the concentration of synagogues in Golan and Galilee, the center of Judaism in Palestine following the Second Revolt against Rome.

amining these synagogues provides the reader insight into the diversity which was characteristic of the architecture and ornamentation of the synagogues of ancient Palestine. Sensitivity to this diversity can lead to an appreciation of early Judaism as the polychromatic phenomenon that it was. Too often what Christians know of early Judaism is based on the obviously polemic portraits presented in the Gospels and patristic works. Acquaintance with the material remains of early Judaism that archaeology has recovered can give a more balanced impression.

Another criterion for selecting the synagogues considered throughout this work was the goal of raising reader awareness of the problems which arise when interpreting the archaeological data and using them to develop an accurate picture of early Judaism. One of the most serious problems of interpretation is the question of the origins of the synagogue—a question which has not yet been resolved. Whether or not a particular building is as a synagogue is often still a controverted issue. In addition, few synagogues in Palestine are securely dated. In fact, only three have inscriptions which even mention dates. Finally, another unresolved problem in the study of ancient synagogues is the question of the propriety of representational art. What is acceptable art and what is not? What criteria did Jews of antiquity use when they decorated their places of worship? Not all of these questions have been resolved to the satisfaction of every scholar; yet it is important for readers to appreciate how complex were the people who are their spiritual ancestors—those who sought to honor by their humble and magnificent synagogues the same God we worship.

The Origins of the Synagogue

For the last two millennia the synagogue has been *the* central institution of Judaism; yet it is doubtful that the synagogue existed within the religion of ancient Israel. Toward the end of the biblical period, legitimate worship came to be confined to the Temple of Jerusalem that the Israelites believed to be the unique dwelling place of their God who was served by an hereditary priesthood. The priests offered prescribed sacrifices intended primarily to insure the fertility of the land. The development of the synagogue marked a genuine religious revolution. Because of the synagogue, worship was no longer centralized at a single site. The synagogue brought liturgical worship to every Jewish village in Palestine. The divinity was symbolically present in the assembly of lay worshippers who followed in their worship a standard ritual which included prayers and readings from the Scriptures, but did not involve sacrifice. Finally, the goal of worship in the synagogue was centered on the salvation of individual worshippers who were praying for the grace of resurrection in the messianic age.

Despite the pivotal importance of the synagogue in the transition from the religion of ancient Israel to that of early Judaism, the origins of the synagogue are a subject of continued controversy. Rabbinic tradition, of course, locates the beginnings of the synagogue in the Mosaic period. The rabbis believed that the synagogue was a divinely ordained institution that owed its existence to God's decree given through Moses and not to any socio-political and religious forces. This belief served to legitimate what was actually an innovation in Jewish worship.[2]

Sherira ben Hanina, a tenth-century C.E. rabbi, was the first to question the Mosaic origins of the synagogue. He suggested that synagogue worship began during the Babylonian Exile.[3] The same hypothesis was advocated and popularized by the sixteenth-century Italian humanist Carlo Sigonio.[4] Until recent archaeological work, this hypothesis was generally accepted by most experts on early Judaism, such as Louis Finkelstein, George Foot Moore, and Samuel Sandmel.[5] They assumed that the fall of Jerusalem and the exile of many of its inhabitants in 587 B.C.E. created a void that the exiles in Babylon filled with prayer meetings instituted by prophets such as Ezekiel (see Ezek 14:1-5). Ezekiel 11:16 is cited as proof of the existence of an exilic synagogue: "Therefore say, 'Thus says the Lord God: Though I removed them far off among the nations, and though I scattered them among the countries, yet I have been a sanctuary to them for a while in the countries where they have gone.' " There are others who agree that the beginnings of the synagogue ought to be located in the Babylonian Exile, but its consolidation was due to Ezra who urged the returning Jews to establish synagogues in Judah.[6]

---

[2] *Targum Pseudo-Jonathan,* Exodus 20:18; *Mekhilta de Rabbi Ishmael,* Amalek 3,174. Acts 15:21 seems to reflect this tradition as well. Both Philo (*The Life of Moses* 3.17) and Josephus (*Contra Apion* 2.17.75) affirm that the synagogue goes back to Moses.

[3] Joseph Gutmann, "Synagogue Origins: Theories and Facts," *Ancient Synagogues: The State of the Research,* Brown Judaic Studies 22 (Chico, Calif.: Scholars Press, 1981) 1.

[4] *De republica Hebraeorum* 7 (Francofurti, 1583) 86.

[5] Louis Finkelstein, "The Origin of the Synagogue," *Proceedings of the American Academy for Jewish Research* 1 (1928-30), 49–59; reprinted in Gutmann, *The Synagogue* (New York: KTAV, 1975) 3–13. See also G. F. Moore, *Judaism in the First Centuries of the Christian Era* (New York: Schocken, 1971) 1:283; and S. Sandmel, *Judaism and Christian Beginnings* (New York: Oxford University Press, 1978) 143.

[6] William Oscar Emil Oesterley, *A History of Israel* (Oxford: Clareudon Press, 1934) 2:138. For others who support this view see I. Sonne, "Synagogue," *Interpreter's Dictionary of the Bible* 4:479.

There is another view which places the origin of the synagogue even earlier—in the seventh century during the Josianic Reform. Part of that reform involved the destruction of the local shrines (2 Kgs 23:8) to ensure that sacrificial worship take place only in Jerusalem. People outside the city of Jerusalem were thus deprived of a place to worship. The practical difficulties involved in making pilgrimages to Jerusalem, and the proscription of sacrificial worship outside the Temple, led to the transformation of local sanctuaries into places of communal prayer without sacrifices. Psalm 74:8 ("they burned all the meeting places of God in the land") is seen as a reference to the newly emerging institution—the synagogue.[7]

Though there was a general consensus among scholars regarding a pre-exilic or exilic date for the origin of the synagogue, there was at least one scholar who proposed a post-exilic date: Solomon Zeitlin.[8] He saw the origin of the synagogue in the secular assemblies of Jews who gathered in their towns and villages to deal with the social and economic problems that faced their communities.[9] As these meetings became more regular, the rabbis introduced the public reading of the Torah for the benefit of those assembled. According to Zeitlin this was the *seed* of the synagogue as an institution. This seed came into fruition with the Pharisaic system of dividing the people into twenty-four divisions which enabled the daily sacrifice in the Temple to be a communal sacrifice provided, in turn, by each of the divisions.

Previously, the daily sacrifice was a private offering made by wealthy Jews who could afford the purchase of the animals prescribed for the sacrifice. When a particular division was responsible for the daily sacrifice, not all its members were able to go to Jerusalem for the ritual. Those who could not remained in their towns and assembled at the time of the sacrifice for prayer and the reading of a passage of Torah relating to the sacrifice. When the Romans destroyed the Temple in 70 C.E., the local divisions continued to meet for prayer and Scripture reading. Thus, what originally was a secular meeting dealing with social and economic questions, became, over the years, a time for prayer with a standardized liturgy.

---

[7] Supporting a preexilic origin for the synagogue is Jacob Weingreen, "The Origin of the Synagogue," *Hermathena* 98 (1964); reprinted in his *From Bible to Mishna* (Manchester: University of Manchester Press, 1976) 115–28. For others, see Joseph Gutmann, "Deuteronomy: Religious Reformation or Iconoclastic Revolution?" *The Image and the Word: Confrontations in Judaism, Christianity and Islam* (Missoula: Scholars Press, 1977) 5–7, 16.

[8] See his "The Origin of the Synagogue" in *Proceedings of the American Academy for Jewish Research* 2:69-81 (1930–31), reprinted in Gutmann, 1975, 14–26.

[9] For example, the meeting called by Joseph, the son of Tobias, to discuss the taxation imposed by the Ptolemies. See Josephus, *Antiquities* 12.4.2.

One of Zeitlin's students, Ellis Rivkin, agreed with his teacher that the synagogue was a post-exilic development, but he saw its origin as part of the Pharisaic response to the crisis within Judaism following the Hasmonean revolt in the second century B.C.E. Pharisaism offered an alternative to the priestly religion of the time with its sacrificial worship offered by hereditary priests at the central shrine. The Pharisees refocused the religious quest on individuals and their salvation. The way to achieve salvation, it was believed, was through obedience to the Torah, the revealed will of God. The synagogue arose as a meeting place where readings and discussions of the Torah took place. In the course of time, these meetings developed the regular patterns of prayer and Scripture reading that characterize the synagogue service.[10]

Another hypothesis assumes that the synagogue cannot refer to a place of formal worship in Judea before the destruction of the Temple in 70 C.E., because it is only after this date that the term *synagogue* is used in connection with a formal liturgical service. Prior to this time, the city square was the locus of public worship outside the Temple.[11] The city square was not only a locus of economic and social life but it was also a center of religious life. The destruction of the Temple provided the catalyst for the development of the synagogue from an assembly in the city square into a religious assembly gathered in a specially designated building.

The problem with these theories regarding the origin of the synagogue is that they are all based on arguments from silence. The Hebrew Scriptures make no mention of a *bet ha-knesset*, the Hebrew equivalent of the Greek word *synagogue*. The Septuagint (the second century B.C.E. translation of the Hebrew Bible into Greek) never uses the term *synagogue* to refer to a building but rather to a liturgical or secular assembly of the people. Even second century B.C.E. Jewish sources, such as Ben Sira and the *Letter of Aristeas*, do not mention synagogues.[12] The synagogue is well attested in Josephus (a first century C.E. Jewish historian) and the New Testament, both first century C.E. sources, but the origins of the synagogue cannot be established from written sources alone.

[10] For bibliographic references see Gutmann 1975, 75, nos. 14 and 15. Gutmann evaluates Rivkin's theory to be the most plausible.

[11] Sidney B. Hoenig, "The Ancient City-Square: The Forerunner of the Synagogue," *Aufstieg und Niedergang der Römischen Welt* (Berlin: Walter de Gruyter, 1979) 2.19.1, 448–48.

[12] See also Ellis Rivkin, "Ben Sira and the Nonexistence of the Synagogue," *In the Time of Harvest: Essays in Honor of Abba Hillel Silver*, ed. D. J. Silver (New York: KTAV 1963); and "Pharisaism and the Crisis of the Individual in the Greco-Roman World," *Jewish Quarterly Review* 60 (1970) 27–53.

It is rather unlikely that the prophet Ezekiel was responsible for instituting the synagogue since his primary concern was the restoration of the Temple (see Ezek 40–48). It is clear from the Bible that Ezekiel's dreams were brought to fulfillment when the Temple was rebuilt and its elaborate sacrificial system was reinstituted under a priestly hierarchy. That the prophet would have been responsible for establishing an institution to rival the Temple is quite improbable. The gatherings of the exiles by Ezekiel were meant not to establish a new pattern of worship for Israel but to keep alive the memories of and hopes for a restoration of the Temple. Also, there is no evidence that the returned exiles met in synagogue-like prayer gatherings. What happened to the synagogue that was supposedly instituted in Babylon? Could it have disappeared until the first century C.E.?

It is even more unlikely that the synagogue was an outcome of the Josianic Reform. The local shrines which were suppressed during Josiah's reform were not transformed into sites where synagogue worship took place. On the contrary, shortly after Josiah's death, the local shrines once again became places of sacrificial worship.[13] Finally, even if meeting places existed either in Babylon during the Exile or in Judah after the restoration, there is no compelling reason to identify these meeting places with synagogues.

There are dedicatory inscriptions from Jewish buildings in Egypt from the third century B.C.E. that some historians accept as proof for the existence of synagogues by that time. These inscriptions refer to a *proseuche* (prayer house).[14] The *proseuche* has been identified with the synagogue. There have, however, been challenges to this identification.[15] The *proseuche* was probably a shrine where prayers were offered to the emperor in the place his statue was erected and worshipped. The term *proseuche* was also used to identify non-Jewish shrines as well, whereas the term *synagogue* was used exclusively for Jewish places of assembly. The actual function of the *proseuche* is still an open question, so identification of these buildings with synagogues must remain uncertain. From what is known it does not appear that the goals and functions of the *proseuche* and the synagogue were the same.

Since written sources do not provide any information about the origin of the synagogue, our only recourse is to consider the material remains that archaeology has revealed. Before we can appreciate ar-

---

[13] Gutmann, *The Image of the Word,* 14.

[14] See Martin Hengel, "Proseuche und Synagogue," *Tradition und Glaube,* eds. G. Jeremias, H. W. Kuhn, and H. Stegemann (Göttingen: Vandenhoeck und Ruprecht, 1971) 157–83. Reprinted in Gutmann 1975, 27–54.

[15] Gutmann, *The Image of the Word,* 74.

chaeology's contribution to resolving this issue, it is important to note that there are two fundamental problems of methodology in the archaeology of ancient synagogues in Palestine: (1) identifying a particular structure as a synagogue, and (2) dating the structure. Sometimes, a building will be identified as a synagogue on the basis of its architectural form or decorative motifs. This evidence, in turn, is used to establish the date of the building. Very few synagogues in Palestine are dated with certainty from inscriptions, and none before the sixth century C.E. Attempting to date a building solely on the basis of its architectural forms and decorative motifs is little more than a guessing game because of the variety of these forms and motifs adopted by Jewish communities in Palestine during the Roman and Byzantine periods.

Despite these difficulties, widely accepted archaeological evidence supports the conclusion that distinct synagogue buildings existed by the third century C.E. These buildings were adaptations of the Roman basilica. In order to correctly identify a particular ruin as the remains of an ancient synagogue, its architectural fragments must be decorated with common Jewish motifs like the Torah shrine or the menorah (the seven-branched candlestick). Sometimes, it is possible to make this identification on the basis of inscriptions that confirm the building's use as a place for liturgical assembly. Neither a building's plan nor its location in a Jewish village is enough to qualify a particular ruin as a synagogue.

Though both Josephus and the New Testament speak of the synagogue as a building or place of Jewish assembly, no building dating from the first century has been positively identified as a synagogue on the basis of the above criteria. The explanation usually given for archaeology's failure to locate synagogues from the first century is that all such buildings were destroyed during the two Jewish revolts against Rome (67–70 and 132–135 C.E.), and their ruins, therefore, are no longer identifiable.

Recent projects have uncovered the remains of structures that excavators have identified as first-century synagogues. Yigael Yadin has identified a building in the casemate wall of Masada, the site of Herod's fortress palace in the Judean desert near the Dead Sea, as a synagogue possibly built by Herod for members of his staff but certainly used as such by the Zealots who were holed up at the site during the First Revolt.[16] Another one of Herod's palaces, Herodion, located a few kilometers southeast of Jerusalem, supposedly yielded another first century synagogue. One room in the palace served as a triclinium (an elaborate dining room) for Herod. Supposedly, the Zealots converted it into a

---

[16] Y. Yadin, *Masada* (New York: Random House, 1966) 184.

place of worship when they sought refuge there during the First Revolt. Another alleged synagogue associated with the First Revolt is an assembly building located at Gamla in the Golan. Shmaryahu Guttman asserts that the plan of the building is similar to the synagogues of Masada and Herodion.[17] He also points to the mikveh (ritual bath) near the entrance of the building as additional proof that it was a synagogue. Two Franciscan archaeologists, Virgilio Corbo and Stanislao Loffreda, identify a small building that they excavated in Migdal, located on the western shore of the Sea of Galilee, as a mini-synagogue dated to the early Roman period (63 B.C.–A.D. 70);[18] and in 1926, a building found at Chorazin (no longer locatable) was described as being similar to a synagogue.[19]

Though some archaeologists do not hesitate to identify these five buildings as synagogues, they do so only on the basis of architectural characteristics these buildings supposedly share with synagogues of a later era.[20] More than likely, these buildings were no more than various kinds of assembly halls in which the Jewish people would gather to conduct community business. There is no indication the buildings served any religious purpose or that they were built to conform to any set of specifications which marked them out for liturgical use.

Joseph Gutmann suggests that the buildings used as synagogues in the first century probably cannot be identified as such since they are not distinguishable from domestic architecture.[21] Perhaps the five buildings mentioned previously were used for worship; however, there is no way of determining this merely from their architectural form. It is more likely that before the third century, single-purpose structures, used only as synagogues and created with a unique architectural form, did not exist. Jews in Palestine met for communal prayer and reading of the Scriptures in private homes that may have been

---

[17] Gideon Foerster, "The Synagogues at Masada and Herodion," *Journal of Jewish Art* 3/4 (1977) 6–11.

[18] S. Loffreda, "La citta romana di Magdala," *Studia Hierosolymitana in onore di P. Bellarimino Bagatti* 1, Studi Archeologici. Studii Biblici Franciscani, Collectio Maior 22 (Jerusalem: Studium Biblicum Franciscanum, 1976) 355–78.

[19] See Marilyn J. Chiat, "First-Century Architecture: Methodological Problems," in Gutmann 1981, 50.

[20] Among those who accept the identification of these buildings as synagogues are G. Foerster ("The Synagogues at Masada and Herodion"), and F. Hüttenmeister and G. Reeg (*Die antiken Synagogen in Israel.* 2 vols. [Wiesbaden: L. Reichart 1977]). M. J. Chiat ("First-Century Synagogue Architecture: Methodological Problems" in J. Gutmann, ed., *Ancient Synagogues,* 49–60) has shown why such identifications are more guesswork than scientific conclusions.

[21] Gutmann 1975, x–xi.

modified for that purpose, or in public buildings that were built to accommodate a wide variety of communal functions. Single-purpose buildings erected to replace the worship of the destroyed second Temple was a later development. Yoram Tsafrir believes that the location of Jewish prayer in special buildings was an innovation which took place some time after the second century c.e.[22]

At present, archaeology and available literary sources can establish no firm date for the origin of the synagogue. Though written sources from the first century, such as the Gospels, state that the Jews worshipped in synagogues, it is not clear that these buildings were, in fact, monumental buildings constructed and used primarily for worship. In all likelihood, these "synagogues" were not distinguishable from ordinary domestic architecture. At times, the community may have assembled for prayer in a building that was erected for other public purposes. Prior to the destruction of the Temple in Jerusalem, it is unlikely that any structure was intended to replace or supplement the Temple and its rituals. In fact, at the very beginning of its use the term synagogue referred to a group of people that met for religious purposes outside of the Temple rather than to a specific building.[23] When the Romans destroyed the second Temple and the probability of its restoration appeared remote, then the synagogue came into its own.

The dating of most Palestinian synagogues remains uncertain. Only one synagogue bears an inscription which registers initial construction while two others have inscriptions dating renovations. Each of these dates are in the Byzantine Period. In fact, most of the synagogues excavated in Palestine are dated by their excavators into one of two clusters: the third and fourth centuries (late Roman and early Byzantine periods) and the fifth and sixth centuries (middle and late Byzantine period). Some of the dates given for particular synagogues, even when they are established by archaeology, are not universally accepted. The question of the origin of the synagogue as a Jewish institution, and the date when synagogue buildings were first erected, remain controverted topics.

The Activities of the Synagogue

The synagogue came to be the central institution of Jewish life and religion during the Roman and Byzantine periods. It effected genuine

---

[22] See his "The Byzantine Setting and its Influence on Ancient Synagogues," in Levine 1987, 148–98.

[23] Levine 1987, 9.

changes in the way Jewish religious rituals were carried on. Most obviously, sacrifice was replaced by prayer and Torah study once the synagogue replaced the Temple as the central Jewish liturgical institution. Second, the priesthood had no essential role in the ritual of the synagogue which included all worshippers. The synagogue democratized Jewish worship.

While the synagogue's main function was liturgical, this was not its only role. A great variety of activities took place in the synagogue that testify to the unique role it played in the maintenance of Jewish identity and values in the periods following both the destruction of the Temple in 70 C.E. and the expulsion of the Jews from Jerusalem in 135 C.E. The synagogue was the religious, social, and cultural center of every Jewish community in Palestine during the Roman and Byzantine periods. It is little wonder, then, that the centerpiece of Justinian's anti-Jewish laws was his edict forbidding the building of synagogues.

Very helpful in understanding the role of the synagogue in Jewish community is an inscribed limestone block found in a cistern in Ophel Hill of Jerusalem (see illust. 2). It was found along with other architectural remains arranged very carefully in the cistern. They were not simply dumped there as so much refuse. Their orderly storage suggests that the fragments were being preserved for future restoration

ILLUSTRATION 2. THE THEODOTUS INSCRIPTION FROM JERUSALEM. It has been dated to the first century of the Common Era. The building it describes has not been found.

or to prevent desecration.[24] The inscription written in Greek on the block is dated to the first century C.E.[25] It reads as follows:

> Theodotus, son of Quettenos (Vettenos), priest and archisynagogus, son of an archisynagogus, grandson of an archisynagogus, built this synagogue for the reading of the Law and for the teaching of the commandments, and the hostel and the chambers and the water fittings for the accommodation of those who [coming] from abroad have need of it, of which [synagogue] the foundations were laid by his fathers and the Elders and the Simonides.[26]

Notice that the inscription says nothing about regular communal prayer services. On the basis of information culled from random comments in the New Testament and from early rabbinic sources, apparently regular daily prayers became part of the synagogue's regimen only after the destruction of the Second Temple.[27] The Gospels and other sources mention regular Sabbath services but what these services included is not certain. After the fall of Jerusalem and the destruction of its Temple during the First Revolt, the synagogue became the pre-eminent setting for communal daily prayer in Jewish communities.

One activity that is mentioned in the Theodotus inscription is the "reading of the Law and the teaching of the commandments." The Mishnah makes it clear that the Jewish man was created to study Torah. It is his reason for existence and therefore it ought to be his greatest joy. It is a precondition of holiness: ". . . A brutish man dreads not sin, and an ignorant man cannot be saintly . . ." (M. Aboth 2:6), and "He that has a knowledge of Scripture and Mishnah and right conduct will not soon fall into sin. . . . But he that has no knowledge of Scripture, Mishnah and right conduct has no part in the habitable world" (M. Kiddushin 1:10). The study of the Torah, then, was not merely an intellectual enterprise, for the most intense presence of God in the world, according to the rabbis, was the Torah. To engage in the study of Torah was an act of communion with the Deity.[28] The natural setting for this activity was the community's synagogue. The study of Torah could take on a number of different forms including classes

---

[24] L. Vincent, "Decouverte de la 'Synagogue des Affranchis' Jerusalem," *Revue Biblique* 30 (April 1921) 247.

[25] See Chiat 1982, 202 for the dating of the inscription. That the text is written in Greek indicates that the people of Jerusalem were able to read and appreciate public announcements in that language.

[26] Chiat 1982, 202.

[27] Levine 1982, 3.

[28] For the thorough presentation of this idea see Benedict Thomas Viviano, O.P., *Study as Worship* (Leiden: Brill, 1978).

for children, exposition of the Scriptures at prayer services (see Luke 4:16-30), and especially regular study sessions for adults with local Torah sages.

Synagogues also served as hostels for Jewish travelers. In addition to the Theodotus inscription, there is another which says as much from the synagogue of Er-Ramah, a Galilean site about 12.5 kilometers from modern Zefat:

> In grateful memory of Rabbi Eliezer, son of Teodor, who built this house as a guest house.[29]

It is probable that most Jewish communities allowed the poor, travelers and wandering merchants to use their synagogues for temporary shelter. Rabbinic sources indicate the *hazan*, a synagogue official, sometimes lived in the synagogue complex.[30]

Another communal activity that look place at the synagogue was sharing special meals that were held most probably in connection with the sabbath and holidays. The Jerusalem Talmud mentions a room adjoining the synagogue that was used for study, prayer, honoring the dead, and eating (y Berakot 3:6a). An inscription from the narthex of a fifth century C.E. synagogue at Caesarea Maritima, the capital of Roman and Byzantine Palestine, attests to this use of the synagogue:

> Beryllos the head of the synagogue (?) and the administrator, the son of Iu[s]tus, made the mosaic work of the triclinium from his own means.[31]

The synagogue also served as a general assembly hall where communal meetings could be held. It housed the local law courts that sometimes meted out punishment within the synagogue itself to offenders. Finally, the synagogue sometimes served as a repository for communal funds.

In the Beth Alpha synagogue there is a small cavity cut into the pavement of the apse. It was coated with plaster and covered with flagstones. Marilyn J.S. Chiat suggests that it was used as a genizah (a repository for worn-out or torn Torah scrolls).[32] The cavity appears to be too small for this purpose. More likely it served as a "community safe."[33]

The remains of Palestine's ancient synagogues serve a contemporary function. They provide a source of information about early Juda-

---

[29] Chiat 1982, 49.
[30] Levine 1982, 4.
[31] Chiat 1982, 157.
[32] Chiat 1982, 124.
[33] Jerome Murphy-O'Connor, O.P., *The Holy Land: An Archeological Guide from the Earliest Times to 1700*, new edition (Oxford: Oxford University Press, 1986) 160.

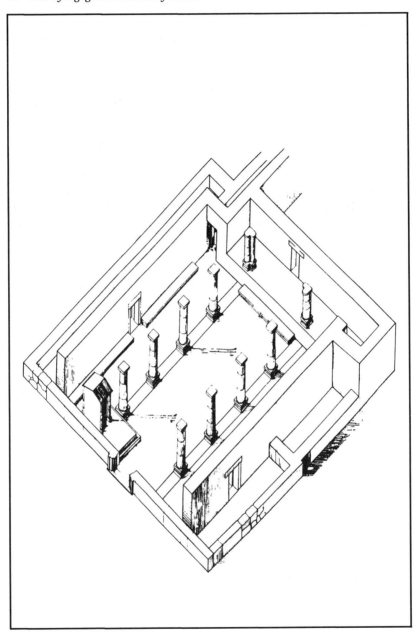

ILLUSTRATION 3. THE PLAN OF A BASILICAL SYNAGOGUE. Note how the two rows of columns divide the interior into a nave and two aisles. Those entering by the main door had to make an awkward about face in order to face the ark resting on the bema which served to direct worship toward Jerusalem.

ism which would otherwise be unavailable. They show that the synagogue provided a place where the people of a Jewish village could engage in almost any kind of communal activity from prayer to banqueting. The synagogue served not only as an assembly space but as a hostel for pilgrims and a repository for communal funds. It was the center for Jewish life.

The Architecture of the Synagogue

Until recently the study of early Judaism has been dominated by George Foot Moore's theory of "normative" Judaism. Moore's hypothesis proposed that "normative" Judaism was a development of the Palestinian and Babylonian rabbinic academies. All other forms of Judaism were considered "fringe" sects.[34] Moore's hypothesis did not appreciate early Judaism as the diverse phenomenon that it was. He overlooked the variety and regional diversity that marked Palestinian Judaism in favor of a model that made early Judaism resemble Christianity with its concern for doctrinal orthodoxy guaranteed by an authoritative hierarchy. The view of early Judaism shaped by Moore's hypothesis made its influence felt in the interpretation of archaeological data to the extent that it appeared as if rabbinic authority was reflected in a "normative" type of synagogue architecture.

The ancient synagogues of Palestine have been classified into three principal types that were usually viewed as stages in a developmental scheme. The first in the scheme is often referred to as the "early," "Galilean" or "basilical" type (see illust. 3). This structure was rectangular in shape with rows of interior columns that served to divide the internal space of the structure and as such it followed the form of the Greco-Roman basilica. Its main entrance was in the wall facing Jerusalem. This necessitated an awkward about-face since worship was directed toward the Holy City. The floors of this type of synagogue were paved with ashlars. The Torah shrine in the basilical synagogue was portable so that it could be moved in and out as needed. A fixed Torah shrine was a feature of the "late" or "apsidal" synagogue (see illust. 4). The apsidal synagogue was the result of an adaptation of the basilical form. The innovation involved the orientation for worship, which was provided by an apse attached to the wall opposite the main entrance. Thus, the need for an about-face was eliminated. Since the apse provided an appropriate setting for the Torah shrine, such shrines became permanent features of the synagogue's internal architecture.

---

[34] See G. F. Moore, *Judaism in the First Centuries of the Christian Era* 2 vols. (New York: Schocken, 1971) [First published in 1927].

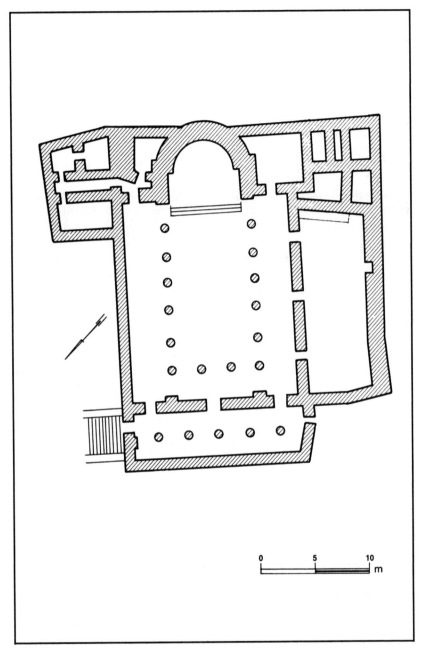

ILLUSTRATION 4. THE PLAN OF A APSIDAL SYNAGOGUE. Note the apse which serves to orient the worship toward Jerusalem, thus eliminating the about turn for those entering by the principal doorway.

The floors of these synagogues were usually paved with mosaics rather than ashlars.

A third type is the broadhouse synagogue which was seen as a transitional form between the early and late types (see illust. 5). The broadhouse followed the rectangular plan of the basilica but the wall orienting the worshipper towards Jerusalem was one of the long walls of the rectangular building.

This three-stage developmental scheme is not very helpful in understanding the synagogues of Palestine since it is based less on the archaeology of these structures than it is on a view of early Judaism which is not accurate.

Another source of this developmental scheme was the work of H. Kohl and C. Watzinger whose book—published in 1916—presented plans of eleven Galilean synagogues.[35] The two archaeologists spent a short time at each of the eleven sites. This did not allow them to engage in excavations adequate to support the conclusions they published. All that they were able to do at each site were some quick probes. Kohl and Watzinger published the field plans that were made after their brief excavations at each site. They also included plans for the restoration of the synagogues. These plans were based on generalizations drawn from the observations of the synagogues. For example, in some restoration plans they show benches even though none were revealed by their excavations.[36] In others, they provide the synagogue with a courtyard along one side of the sanctuary even though only one synagogue (Capernaum) actually shows any evidence of such a courtyard. In the years since Kohl and Watzinger published their report, their hypothetical restoration plans have been reproduced more often than the field reports of their excavations. The conjectures of these two men, made on the basis of a relatively short time spent at each site, became the foundation of a chronological scheme of synagogue architecture that dominated the scholarly literature.

On the basis of recent excavations, it has become clear that the restoration plans of Kohl and Watzinger are misleading. Theoretically, one of the basic features of the "early" synagogue type was that it had two rows of columns running lengthwise and a short row running crosswise opposite the main entrance so that the building's internal space would be divided into a central nave with two side aisles.[37]

---

[35] *Antike Synagogen in Galiläa.* (Leipzig: Hinrichs, 1916).

[36] Benches were used by the elderly and others of frail health. All others would simply sit on mats placed on the floor. Still, not all ancient synagogues had benches.

[37] Eric M. Meyers, "Synagogue, Architecture." *Interpreter's Dictionary of the Bible.* Supplementary Volume, 843.

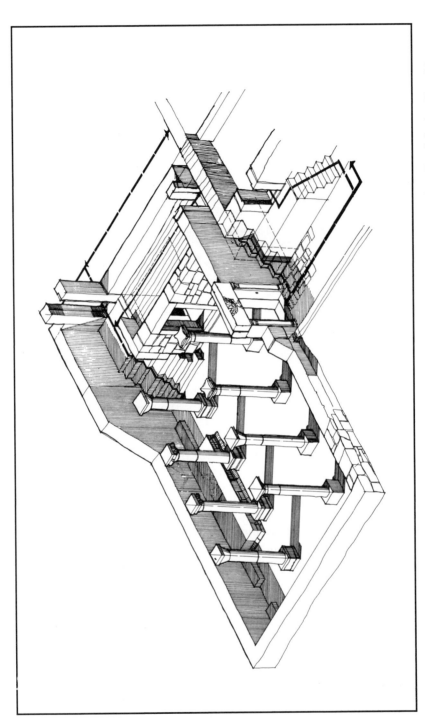

ILLUSTRATION 5. THE PLAN OF A BROADHOUSE SYNAGOGUE. The bema is against one of the broad walls of the basilica. No turn-about was necessary upon entering such a synagogue.

It was assumed that the colonnades served to support a women's gallery. Andrew R. Seager reports that the synagogue at Bar'am in Upper Galilee was restored according to this hypothesis. He maintains that a careful examination of the architectural remains of the synagogue shows that the colonnade was a full peristyle. The columns ran around all four sides of the room at a uniform distance from the walls.[38] There could not have been a women's gallery based on the architectural fragments found. Similarly, the hypothesis of a women's gallery in Galilean synagogues is based more on a retroversion of medieval Jewish custom than on archaeological evidence.[39] It is clear that there was no women's gallery at Capernaum, though one has been suggested on the basis of a few architectural fragments.[40] No indisputable evidence of such a gallery has surfaced in the excavation of any ancient synagogue in Palestine.

Recent excavation of synagogues in Galilee have proven that there is considerable variety in the design of ancient synagogues.[41] Any classification system needs to be sensitive to these differences. A main problem with the traditional classification system is that the various forms of synagogue architecture are related to one another sequentially. Excavations have shown this simply to be incorrect. For example, Meiron and Khirbet Shema' were two Jewish communities in Upper Galilee which were closely linked socially, economically and culturally. Both erected synagogues in the third century c.e. Meiron's synagogue was a basilical type while Khirbet Shema''s was a broadhouse. The synagogue of Capernaum has usually been presented as the archetype of the "early" type. A recent excavation, however, dates this structure to the middle of the fourth or fifth century. Relating the forms of synagogue architecture sequentially does not agree with the archaeological evidence. An alternative approach is to relate the synagogue types regionally. The basilical type is concentrated in a relatively small area in Golan and Galilee.[42] No undisputed examples are found elsewhere. Similarly, the apsidal synagogues are found farther south.

Once the basilical synagogues are seen as a localized phenomenon, it is possible to see regionalism as an important element in the

---

[38] Gutman 1981, 40–41.

[39] S. S. Safrai, "Was There a Women's Galley in the Synagogue of Antiquity?" *Tabriz* 32 (1963) 329–38 [Hebrew with English summary].

[40] E. L. Sukenik, *Ancient Synagogues in Palestine and Greece* (London: Oxford University Press, 1934) 7–21, 52–53.

[41] Eric M. Meyers, "The Current State of Galilean Synagogue Studies" (Levine 1987, 127–37).

[42] Gutmann 1981, 39–48.

process of understanding early Judaism.[43] Galilee, for example, is composed of two different regions. The smaller of the two (180 square miles) is Upper Galilee, defined by the slopes of Mount Meiron—the highest mountain in Israel proper. The much larger region of Lower Galilee (470 square miles) is bordered on the north by the southern slope of Mount Meiron; on the south by the Nazareth fault to Mount Tabor where it turns north to the southern end of the Sea of Galilee: on the east by the Sea of Galilee; and on the west by the Mount Carmel.[44]

Lower Galilee offered no natural barrier to communication, and so this region was affected by the busy trade between the Mediterranean region and the area surrounding the Sea of Galilee. It was marked by a more cosmopolitan sense. In contrast, Upper Galilee was isolated by its topography. It was less affected by the increasing aesthetical sensitivity that was developing in the Jewish communities in Lower Galilee. Upper Galilee's regional conservatism is obvious when a comparison is made between its synagogues—such as Meiron, Gush Halav, Nabratein, and Khirbet Shema'—and those of Lower Galilee—such as Capernaum, Chorazin, Hamat Tiberias, and Beth Alpha. The former are almost without any decorative elements, while the latter show ornate decoration of architectural elements and some beautiful mosaic floors.[45] Attempts at understanding early Judaism need to take seriously the phenomenon of regionalism which points to the diversity of religious thought, practice and expression. The archaeology of ancient synagogues in Palestine testifies eloquently to this phenomenon. Using literary sources alone to paint the picture of early Judaism has led to distortions and misunderstandings. Archaeology makes available the material culture of early Judaism which can help fill out the picture sketched by the literary sources.

One conclusion which is inevitable from a study of these material remains is that early Judaism was marked by diversity. Judaism's sur-

---

[43] On regionalism see Eric M. Meyers, "The Cultural Setting of Galilee: The Case for Regionalism and Early Judaism," *Aufstieg und Niedergang der Römischen Welt* II.19.1, 686–702; and his "Galilean Regionalism as a Factor in Historical Reconstruction," *Bulletin of the American Schools of Oriental Research* 221 (1976) 93–101.

[44] Though neither the Hebrew Scriptures nor the New Testament mention this division, it is clear that such a division goes back to the Hellenistic period (fourth century B.C.E.). Tobit 1:2 and Judith 1:7-8 assume this division and Josephus mentions it explicitly in *Antiquities* 5:63, 86, 92. For additional information see Eric M. Meyers and James F. Strange, *Archeology, the Rabbis and Early Christianity* (Nashville: Abingdon, 1981) 179, no. 17.

[45] The same phenomenon is evident in the Jewish necropolis at Beth She'arim in Lower Galilee. Here Hellenistic artistic motifs and Greek inscriptions are predominant. This necropolis was in use from the third to the seventh centuries C.E.

vival to the present day bespeaks of a diversity and flexibility which contributes to that survival. The ancient synagogues of Palestine show that these qualities have marked Judaism from the very beginning.

Chapter 2

Two Galilean Synagogues

Introduction

Galilee, the region Jesus called home, is not a single geographical region. Jesus was from Nazareth, the center of Lower Galilee, and most of his Galilean ministry was located in the area around the Sea of Galilee. When Jesus wanted to be alone and away from the crowds, he would slip into Upper Galilee (e.g., Mark 7:24; 8:27). In Jesus' day, this area was only lightly populated. After the two unsuccessful Jewish revolts against Rome, the population of this region swelled with Jewish refugees from Jerusalem and its environs. Jews from Judea came to Upper Galilee in order to live in an area that was somewhat out of the way and not overwhelmed with the presence of the Roman legions as Jerusalem and Judah were. By the end of the second century C.E., the center of Judaism in Palestine shifted from Judea to Galilee. Rabbinic academies were established there; and in the one located in Sepphoris, the main city of Lower Galilee, Rabbi Judah the Prince completed his edition of the Mishnah around 200 C.E. To understand the development of rabbinic Judaism, then, one must be familiar with Galilee, its history and archaeology.

Until the 1970s the work of most archaeologists excavating in Palestine was confined almost exclusively to sites connected with the Hebrew Scriptures and the history of ancient Israel. Sites associated with Christian origins and the rise of rabbinic Judaism did not receive as much attention since it was thought that literary sources provided enough information about early Judaism and Christianity. Also, students of the New Testament focused their attention on the theological concerns of the Christian Scriptures and considered the historical, archaeological, and sociological dimensions secondary and tangential. The current growing interest in the social milieu from which the Church emerged will result in more attention to the kind of data that archaeology can supply.[1] There has been a similar bias in favor of literary sources among those who study the origins of rabbinic Judaism. This exclusive reliance on texts has led to an oversimplified portrait of early Judaism that scholars today recognize to be a very complex and diverse phenomenon—a conclusion derived, in no small measure, from the work of archaeologists. In the study of early Christianity and rabbinic Judaism, the use of literary *and* material sources will yield a more comprehensive understanding of the culture which gave rise to these two great faiths.

The Synagogue of Nabratein

Naturally, Upper Galilee has a magnetic attraction to anyone interested in probing the origins of rabbinic Judaism. From 1971 to 1981, three American archaeologists, Eric M. Meyers, James F. Strange and Carol L. Meyers, began a systematic study of the region with surveys and a full-scale excavation of the synagogues at four sites in Upper Galilee: Khirbet Shema', Meiron, Gush Halav, and Nabratein. Their Meiron Excavation Project has served as a model of how important the study of a region's material culture can be. The site under discussion in this section is Nabratein, located about four kilometers north of the modern city of Zefat (Safed).[2] Nabratein is the Arabic name for a town mentioned in the Jerusalem Talmud and other early Jewish sources such as Neburaya (see y. Yebamouth II.5; Pesikta Rabbathi 14; Genesis Rabbah 7.23, par. 3). These sources name Neburaya as the home of a fourth century rabbi and popular preacher named Jacob who is described as "a sinner" (Midrash Ecclesiastes Rabbah 7:26, par. 3). This may indicate that he became a Christian. A few medieval Jewish texts also mention this site.

The ruins of Nabratein's synagogue were discovered in the late nineteenth century by both Charles Wilson and Ernest Renan who noted the presence of an inscribed lintel among the architectural fragments on the site (see illust. 6).[3] Apart from a three day period in 1905

---

[1] For a review of recent literature see Carolyn Osiek, R.S.C.J., *What Are They Saying about the Social Setting of the New Testament?* (New York: Paulist, 1984).

[2] E. M. Meyers, J. F. Strange, and C. L. Meyers, "Preliminary Report on the 1981 Excavations at en-Nabratein, Israel," *Bulletin of the American Schools of Oriental Research* 224 (Fall 1981) 1–26; and "Second Preliminary Report on the 1981 Excavations at en-Nabratein, Israel," *Bulletin of the American Schools of Oriental Research* 246 (Spring 1982) 35–54.

[3] C. R. Conder and H. H. Kitchener, *A Survey of Western Palestine*, vol. 1, *Galilee* (London: Palestine Exploration Fund, 1881) 244 [reprinted by Kedem Press in Jerusalem, 1970].

when Kohl and Watzinger sunk some probe trenches and recorded some now lost architectural fragments, no excavations were attempted at Nabratein until 1980 when the Meiron Excavation Project began its work.

The most interesting discovery from the early surveys of the ruins at Nabratein was the inscribed limestone lintel. This lintel is a little over two meters long. In its center is an inscription of some seventy-five letters, most of which are in relief, though a few are incised into the limestone. Topping off the lintel is a frieze decorated with laurel leaves. Though the inscription on the lintel was publicized a number of times in the early part of this century, it was not actually deciphered until 1960 by Nahum Avigad.[4] The inscription reads as follows: "(According) to the number four hundred and ninety-four years after the destruction (of the Temple), the house was built during the office of Hanina son of Lezer and Luliana son of Yudan."

The date on the lintel is equivalent to 564 C.E., a date that is problematic on both historical and architectural grounds. First, the imperial policy in the Byzantine period severely restricted the freedom of the Jews even in Palestine. In 545 Emperor Justinian reconfirmed earlier laws that prohibited the building of any new synagogues. In addition, this era witnessed forced conversions of Jews, the desecration of synagogues, and other forms of persecution. These imperial policies were responsible for the growth of animosity between Christians and Jews in Palestine, and occasionally this animosity spilled over into violence, as it did in 556 when the Jews and Samaritans rioted against Byzantine rule. In the wake of these tensions and events, it is highly unlikely that the people of Nabratein would have been able to erect a synagogue in 564.[5] Second, the lintel itself and other architec-

[4] See Meyers, Strange, and Meyers, "Preliminary Report," 4.

[5] The excavators of the synagogue at Capernaum dates it from 450–50. If they are correct, it was not impossible for Jews to build synagogues in Palestine despite the anti-Jewish laws of the Byzantine empire. See note 11 below.

ILLUSTRATION 6. THE LINTEL OF THE NABRATEIN SYNAGOGUE. Note the menorah in the center and the inscription.

tural fragments found along with it reflect the style of the later Roman period (250–350 C.E.) rather than the Byzantine period. Avigad suggested that the lintel was part of a building constructed in the late Roman period which was simply being renovated in sixth century. The inscription, then, commemorated the renovation rather then the construction of the synagogue itself.[6] One objective of the Meiron Excavation Project's work was to test Avigad's hypothesis explaining the anomaly of a sixth-century date found on what appeared to be a lintel from at least two hundred years earlier.

The very first season of work did, in fact, confirm Avigad's hypothesis that there was a Byzantine period renovation of a synagogue which was originally constructed at an earlier date. The second season's work clarified the synagogue's history. The first synagogue built at the site excavated in Nabratein dates from the middle Roman period (135–250). It was a broadhouse synagogue whose external dimensions were 11.2 by 9.35 meters. Its roof was probably supported by two rows of columns, though the building was small enough to obviate the need for such support. The floor of this rather simple building was plastered. On either side of the southern entrance to the synagogue, there were two stone platforms. One of these was probably the synagogue's bema (a podium from which the Scriptures were read); the other served to support the ark in which the sacred scrolls were kept. Stone benches were found along the eastern and western walls.

This rather small structure evidently served the needs of the village until it grew in population and prosperity at the beginning of the late Roman period in the middle of the third century. Rather than constructing an entirely new building on a different site, the people of Nabratein simply enlarged their first synagogue by moving its northern wall by 4.5 meters. This increased its area by forty-eight percent and converted the building to a basilica. Two rows of three columns each were installed on stylobates. The floor was raised in the process of resurfacing and a stone aedicula was erected on the western bema. A fragment of this ark was discovered reused upside down in the rebuilt bema of a later period of synagogue usage. The lintel *without* the later inscription dates from this renovation.

The beautiful lintel was not the only decorative element that adorned this synagogue. There was a surprising number of animal sculptures at Nabratein. Evidently, the villagers at Nabratein did not interpret the biblical prohibition of images (Exod 20:4; Deut 5:8) to include all

---

[6] N. Avigad, "A Dated Lintel-Inscription from the Ancient Synagogue of Nabratein," *Louis M. Rabinowitz Fund for the Exploration of Ancient Synagogues Bulletin* III (1960) 55.

representational art. The lions, eagles, and other animal figures that decorated this synagogue are a striking exception to the general pattern found elsewhere in the synagogues of Upper Galilee. Synagogues such as Khirbet Shema' and Meiron were devoid of the kind of representational art that the people of Nabratein evidently found quite acceptable.

An earthquake struck in Palestine in 306 and caused severe damage to the synagogue at Nabratein. The building was immediately rebuilt. This project consisted in laying a new floor, strengthening the two bemas that flanked the main entrance. Incorporated in one of the rebuilt bemas was the damaged ark fragment. This was done to show reverence to the damaged ark. Even the tiles from the roof destroyed by the earthquake were carefully buried under the floor of the synagogue. One did not simply discard objects made holy by their use in a place of worship. This rebuilt late Roman synagogue served the village for just over fifty years. In 363, another earthquake struck the region but this time repairs were not made on the building since the village was dying and was virtually abandoned by 370. The probable cause for the wane of Nabratein and other Jewish villages in the Upper Galilee was the excessive taxation of Constantius II. Thus, economic hardship made worse by natural disaster led the people to disperse.

Village life in Nabratein resumed in the sixth century and so it was necessary for the synagogue to be rebuilt. The villagers once again enlarged their place of worship. It may have been that the population in the Byzantine period was larger than that of the Roman period or that the villagers simply wanted to have a substantial house of worship as was the fashion of the day. In any case, the building was enlarged by another twenty-one percent. It now measured 11.2 by 16.8 meters. Its stylobates were extended to support two rows of columns with four columns each. The floor had to be raised in order to make it level with the higher level of bedrock at its northern end. The bemas were not rebuilt and there is no structural evidence for a permanent Torah shrine. The floor was made of flagstone pavers founded on cobbles which had been laid into plaster. The lintel from the Roman period was inscribed when the third synagogue was built and it dates this reconstruction with precision to 564. A gold coin of Justinian I was found immediately below the threshold of the doorway. It was probably placed there deliberately in connection with the reconstruction work and confirms Avigad's hypothesis about the lintel and its inscription. The synagogue was in use until 700 when the people of Nabratein abandoned their village once again.

There were, then, four phases of the synagogue's history. The first building was a broadhouse erected at the end of the second or the early part of the third century. Around 250, the building was expanded into a basilica and was in use until 306 when an earthquake did substantial damage. After being repaired quickly, the synagogue remained in use until the village was abandoned around 370. No reconstruction of the building was attempted until a sizable population returned to Nabratein in the middle of the sixth century. The village and its synagogue were abandoned for the last time at the beginning of the eighth century.

The discovery of the fragment of the late Roman synagogue's Torah shrine was certainly fortunate since Nabratein's ark is the only ark to have been discovered from any synagogue of antiquity in Palestine. The fragment is 1.30 meters high, .58 meter high, and .50 meter thick. Of course, in its undamaged state it would have been much larger. All that remains is the top part of the aedicula (see illust. 7). The center of the ark is decorated with a scallop-shell carving, .36 meter in radius. Above the shell is a gabled roof decorated with egg-and-dart molding. Between the molding and the shell are at least two rosettes. Above the gables are two rampant lions. These motifs are common to Jewish art from Palestine and the Diaspora of the Greco-Roman period. Just below the central rosette, there is a small hole which had been drilled into molding above the shell. Presumably, this hole was made to accommodate a chain to hold the lamp which was always burning in front of the scrolls housed in a synagogue. This hole served to confirm the identity of the fragment as a portion of an ark. No other arks survived from the synagogues of ancient Palestine because, presumably, these arks were made of wood which decomposed over the centuries. The limestone ark of Nabratein survived very well the vagaries of time.

The significance of Nabratein's ark cannot be overestimated. This is material evidence for the high regard that the Jews of third century Galilee had for the scrolls of the Torah. The ark of the synagogue served as the spiritual successor of the Temple's ark of the covenant that was the symbol of the divine presence in the Temple. The decorative motifs of the ark fragment show that the villagers of Nabratein were as much at home in the Roman world as they were in the world of their ancient Israelite ancestors. The rampant lions, especially, prove that they felt no hesitation about the use of representational art even in connection with this most sacred object. The ark of the Nabratein synagogue testifies to the transformation of the synagogue from a place of assembly to a house of worship where the divine might be encountered through prayerful reading of the Scriptures. The ark of Nabratein, and the synagogue which housed it, represents a powerful reminder of the human quest for the Divine.

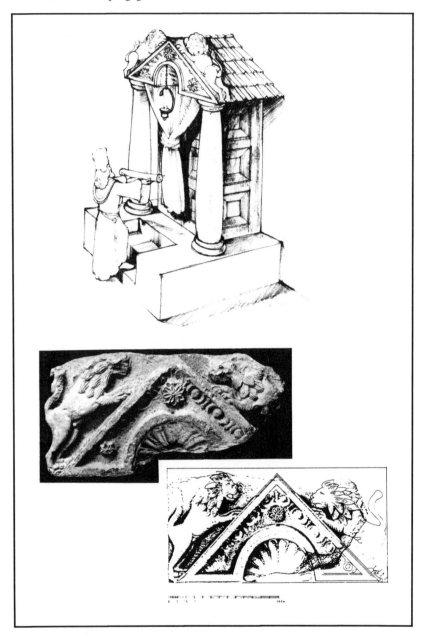

ILLUSTRATION 7. THE ARK OF NABRATEIN. In the center is a photograph of the pediment of the ark. Below the photograph is an artist's rendition of the fragment. Above both is an artistic reconstruction of the ark as it may have appeared in the synagogue.

The Synagogue of Capernaum

Capernaum is located on the northwestern shore of the Sea of Galilee. Matthew states that Jesus moved from Nazareth to Capernaum when he began his ministry (Matt 4:13). Such a move is quite understandable since Nazareth was a tiny, unimportant village (see John 1:46) while Capernaum was a relatively large town with a population approaching fifteen thousand.[7] The town's size can be explained by its location along an important trade route. It was located on a branch of the Via Maris that connected the area surrounding the Sea of Galilee with Golan and Syria. Capernaum was important enough to be a center for the collection of taxes (see Mark 2:14). The Gospels mention the town sixteen times and present it as the hub of Jesus' Galilean ministry. While Matthew simply states that Jesus traveled throughout Galilee to teach in its synagogues (4:23), Mark mentions the synagogue of Capernaum by name as one of the places where Jesus taught (1:21). The other two evangelists are even more specific. Luke identifies the town's synagogue as the site of an exorcism performed by Jesus (4:31-37), and John names it as the location of Jesus' discourse on the bread of life (6:59). John also notes that the reaction to this discourse on the part of many of Jesus' disciples was quite negative and it became the cause of their defection (6:60, 66). Matthew (11:23-24) and Luke (10:15) state that Jesus cursed Capernaum for its failure to respond to his call of repentance. This town, then, was the site of some of Jesus' greatest triumphs as well as his greatest disappointments.

The name "Capernaum" is a corruption of the Hebrew phrase *kfar Nahum*, i.e., "the village of Nahum." Since the town is never mentioned in the Hebrew Bible and archaeological evidence dates its earliest occupation to the late Hellenistic period (second century, B.C.E.), it is unlikely that this "Nahum" was the ancient Israelite prophet. The association made between the biblical Nahum and Capernaum by medieval Jewish sources is without historical basis. The town probably was named after the original owner of the land on which it was built, though this is only conjecture. Josephus wrote that he found refuge in the town after he was wounded during the course of the First Revolt against Rome (*Vita* 403); otherwise, Capernaum took no part in that revolt. Talmudic sources relate that a Christian community existed in Capernaum by the second century. The town was rather prosperous because it was a center for trade with regions to the north and east of Galilee. Other sources of prosperity were agriculture and fishing. Capernaum was destroyed in the seventh century and was never rebuilt, though

---

[7] Meyers and Strange 1981, 58.

a thirteenth century writer notes that a few poor fishermen and their families lived there.

Archaeological study of this site began in 1857 when Edward Robinson surveyed the ruins at the site and correctly identified the visible architectural fragments as belonging to a synagogue. Charles Wilson of the London-based Palestine Exploration Fund began a small-scale excavation at the site in 1866. He was the first to identify the site as that of ancient Capernaum and concluded that the synagogue he surveyed was the very one built by the Roman centurion mentioned in Luke 7:5, and the one in which Jesus preached.[8] Additional work on the site was done by H. H. Kitchener in 1881. The interest shown by these foreigners in the ruins of ancient Capernaum peaked the interest of the local population who thought they might find some treasure at the site or at least some small artifacts to sell on the local antiquities market. Also, once the site was cleared and its architectural fragments exposed, local contractors began looting the site for stones to be used in their own construction projects. Fortunately, this was stopped once the site was acquired by the Franciscan Custody of the Holy Land in 1894. Among the practical steps the friars took to stop the looting of the site was the building of a high wall around the property.

The solicitude of the Franciscans preserved the site and made continued archaeological study possible. Additional work on the synagogue was done by H. Kohl and C. Watzinger in 1905 as part of their important survey of the synagogues of Galilee.[9] From 1905 until 1926, two Franciscan friars—Wendelin Hinterkeuser and Gaudentius Orfali—began excavating in the synagogue area. As they extended their probes, they came upon an octagonal structure to the south of the synagogue, which eventually was identified as a Byzantine period church. Despite this new discovery, the synagogue remained the center of activity. Under the direction of Friar Orfali, work began on the reconstruction of the synagogue. The good number of architectural fragments which remained from the synagogue made it possible to begin modest attempts at restoration—work that is continuing into the present. Recent excavations began in 1968 and continued until 1972 under the direction of the Franciscans Virgilio Corbo and Stanislao Loffreda.[10]

---

[8] C. W. Wilson, *Quarterly Statement of the Palestine Exploration Fund* I (1869) 37–41.

[9] H. Kohl and C. Watzinger, *Antike Synagogen in Galiläa* (Leipzig: H. J. Hinrichs, 1916). This was reprinted by Kedem publishers of Jerusalem in 1973.

[10] Virgilio C. Corbo, *Cafarnao I: Gli Edifici della Citta* (Jerusalem: Franciscan Press, 1975); Stanislao Loffreda, *Cafarnao II: La Ceramica* (Jerusalem: Franciscan Press, 1974); Augusto Spijkermann, *Cafarnao III: Catalogo della Monete della Citta* (Jerusalem: Franciscan Press, 1975).

Though the Gospels mention a synagogue in Capernaum, no such building has been discovered at the site. In fact, the excavators have found no public buildings from the first century at the site. Corbo and Loffreda date the synagogue at the site from the middle of the fourth to the middle of the fifth century. This has caused no little controversy among archaeologists.[11] Early excavators of the synagogue—first Wilson and later Orfali—were each convinced that they had uncovered the building in which Jesus preached. Today, all reputable archaeologists reject a first century date for the synagogue. It may be that there was a monumental building below the Byzantine structure, but there is no conclusive evidence of that yet.

Kohl and Watzinger suggested that Capernaum's synagogue was built in the second century, a date which had been accepted by most archaeologists. In fact, Corbo and Loffreda began with a second-to-third century dating as a working hypothesis. On the basis of numismatic evidence, they had to revise their hypothesis. Although they admitted that they were taken by surprise, the evidence was beyond dispute. Those who reject the conclusion of the two Franciscans interpret the numismatic evidence differently. According to their critics, the coins which Corbo and Loffreda see as providing clear evidence of the synagogue's date were not introduced when the building was being erected but instead while it was undergoing repairs at a much later date. Gideon Foerster holds that the building must be dated to the second century since it reflects a pattern in Roman architecture that is found in the region at that time.[12] Michael Avi-Yonah considers it highly unlikely that a magnificent structure such as the Capernaum synagogue could have been built in the fourth century since the emperors reigning at the time—Constantine and Constantius II—were quite hostile to the Jews.[13]

Avi-Yonah is certainly right about the magnificence of Capernaum's synagogue. The partially reconstructed state of the building makes even the casual contemporary observer marvel (see illust. 8). Its original state certainly must have been breathtaking for its beauty. The building was

---

[11] See Loffreda's essay, "The Late Chronology of the Synagogue of Capernaum," in Levine 1981, 52–56.

[12] Gideon Foerster, "Notes on Recent Excavations at Capernaum," in *Ancient Synagogues Revealed*, 57–59.

[13] Michael Avi-Yonah, "Some Comments on the Capernaum Excavations," *Ancient Synagogues Revealed*, 60–62. Of course, as Avi-Yonah himself suggests, local officials could be persuaded by bribes to ignore official policy. Also, the relationship between Capernaum's Jews and Christians could have been such that the latter would have supported the former's desire for a place to worship.

ILLUSTRATION 8. AN AERIAL VIEW OF CAPERNAUM. The synagogue is in the foreground. The octagonal building in the background is "The House of Peter"; and between these two monumental structures are the remains of private homes.

constructed of large white limestone blocks of hewn stone. Their external surface was polished to imitate the appearance of marble. This white limestone structure stood out from its surroundings since most of the other structures in the town were built using basalt, a black volcanic rock that is abundant in the area. The Jews of Capernaum had to import the limestone at some expense from other areas of Galilee. This, together with the delicately sculpted decorative motifs of the synagogue's architectural components, show that the construction of this synagogue was a very costly project. That the Jews of Capernaum were able to underwrite such a project is an indication of the community's economic prosperity.

The ashlars were set without mortar and their interior surface was left rough in order to receive plaster. Some fragments of painted stucco were found inside the building's main entrance. The floor was covered with stone pavers. The building measures about 24.5 by 18.5 meters. There were lateral stairways on the southwest and southeast corners of the synagogue which ascended from the street level to a terrace that ran the full length of the synagogue and the adjoining courtyard. This terrace was a narrow open porch paved with large smooth slabs of stone.

The courtyard attached to the synagogue on the east had a portico covered on three sides. This courtyard measures 20.4 by 13.3 meters. Unlike the synagogue, it was not perfectly rectangular in shape but trapezoidal. The courtyard and its portico provided open space as well as a shaded area outside the worship space itself for all the diverse activities that normally took place in the environs of the synagogue. This area would have been used for study, trying legal cases, communal meals, and other social gatherings. This extra feature is another indication of the extravagance that marked this building. It had a large central door opening to the south. On the east and north there were three unevenly spaced doors, while there was a single door on the west side which opened to the synagogue's western aisle. The floor was paved with flagstone.

Despite the looting of the site before the Franciscans took control of it, architectural fragments of the synagogue were so numerous as to make possible a hypothetical reconstruction of the building's appearance. The façade faced the south, i.e., toward Jerusalem. Three fields comprised the façade: the lower story, the upper story, and the gabled roof. Three elaborately decorated doorways marked the lower story (see illust. 9). The lintels of these doorways bore carvings of date palms and other fruits, as well as shell motifs, garlands, geometric patterns, and animal figures. The latter were defaced probably by people whose religious sensibilities were offended by any representation of a living creature.[14] A cornice that itself was rich in moldings of various floral and geometric patterns separated the first and second stories. The central feature of the latter was a large arch above the center doorway. This arch framed a window which allowed sunlight to enter the building. On either side of the large central window was a smaller window. Each of these was fashioned to resemble the front of a Torah shrine: two small columns supported a gable with a shell motif in the center. A second cornice, more highly decorated than the first, separated the second story from the gables. The roof was probably covered with terracotta tiles since fragments were found among the debris in the area.

The structure's three front entrances opened to the interior of the synagogue that was arranged in basilical style. Beside the two rows

[14] Similar defacing is in evidence throughout Palestine and is often associated with the Islamic incursions into the area beginning in the seventh century, though Jewish iconoclasts were at work earlier. Islam forbids representational art. Some Jews interpreted the second commandment in such a way as to forbid such art as well, but the evidence of the Capernaum synagogue—among others—shows that there was a diversity in the way this prohibition was understood. See Jacob Neusner, "The Symbolism of Ancient Judaism: The Evidence of the Synagogues," in Gutmann 1981, 7–17.

ILLUSTRATION 9. AN ARTIST'S RENDERING OF THE FACADE OF THE CAPERNAUM SYNAGOGUE.

of columns that divided the interior space of the synagogue into a central nave and two side aisles, there was a third row of columns that served to close the two rows of columns at the northern end of the building, thus creating a third aisle along the back wall of the synagogue. Along the interior walls of the building there were two rows of benches and a "Chair of Moses" (see Matt 23:2), though the identification of the latter is not certain because of its fragmentary state. A similar chair was found at the synagogue of Chorazin. The bases of the columns were of the Attic type (marked by simplicity), while the capitals were of the Corinthian type (marked by highly ornate decorations). Some of the capitals were adorned with Jewish symbols such as the menorah (the candelabra of the Temple), the shofar (the ram's horn trumpet), and the incense shovel. Two of the columns still bear inscriptions, one is in Greek and the other in Aramaic. Both inscriptions name individuals who "built" the particular column. The individuals named were probably benefactors who helped finance the construction of the synagogue.

Another interesting feature of the synagogue's present internal architecture is the frieze, the decorative limestone beam that connects the tops of the columns that make up the lateral row along the north end of the building. The central feature of the frieze is the side view of a wheeled carriage that apparently represents a portable Torah shrine. Such an object contained the scrolls read during the service. The shrine is made to look like an Ionic temple with double-winged doors above which is a scalloped shell. The roof is gabled. Other features on the frieze include two eagles and a goat. The latter may represent one of the signs of the zodiac which is used in a few Palestinian synagogues as a decorative piece. These animal figures on the frieze are the only ones from the synagogue that escaped the hands of the iconoclasts.

There are two features of the building's internal architecture that have not been adequately explained to everyone's satisfaction. A number of small columns and capitals, as well as other architectural fragments, have led Kohl and Watzinger to conclude that there was a second story that served as a women's gallery.[15] Loffreda, however, maintains that the building's foundation could not have supported a second story. The second unexplained feature of the synagogue's interior is the pair of platforms that were built on either side of the main entrance. Corbo simply describes these in his report on the building without suggesting what their use may have been. In his review of the Capernaum volumes, James Strange proposed that these platforms

---

[15] Kohl and Watzinger, *Antike Synagogen in Galilaea,* 14–21.

were built to support two aediculae.[16] One of these shrines would have been the Torah shrine; the other could have supported the menorah. The latter became a standard element of a synagogue's appointments. If Strange's suggestion is correct, the location of these aediculae along the southern wall of the building would have compelled the worshipper to turn around after entering the building from the south. Thus, the worship of the synagogue would have been offered while facing Jerusalem.

The synagogue of Capernaum is perhaps the most beautiful of all that has survived from antiquity in Palestine. When first discovered, it attracted quite a bit of interest because the Gospels mention that Jesus preached in a synagogue in Capernaum (e.g., John 6). Even after it became clear that the ancient structure that has been excavated and partially reconstructed was not standing at the time of Jesus' ministry, Capernaum's synagogue, nonetheless, was a focus of scholarly attention. It became the prototype of the Galilean synagogue and all others were compared to it. It was assumed that it provided the model for other communities in Galilee as they erected their own synagogues. Recently, the synagogue at Capernaum has been the center of a serious controversy. Again, it is a matter of dating. Some archaeologists, out of historical and architectural theories, maintain that the date offered by Corbo and Loffreda cannot be correct. The latter defend their fourth-fifth century date for the synagogue on the basis of stratigraphy—based on evidence, not theories.

Despite these controversies, the synagogue of Capernaum is a delight for the eyes. Reconstruction at the site continues making it possible for visitors to marvel at the aesthetic sense and engineering skill that combined to produce such a strikingly beautiful building. Its size and ornamentation testify not only to the wealth of the Jewish community of ancient Capernaum which constructed it, but also to their devotion to the God of their ancestors.

[16] James F. Strange, "The Capernaum and Herodium Publications," *Bulletin of the American Schools of Oriental Research* 226 (1977) 70.

Chapter 3

The Synagogues of Judea

Introduction: Disputed Synagogues

Though Galilee is rich in synagogues (eighteen validated, seventeen attested and twenty-two disputed), comparatively few ancient synagogues have been found in Judea (six validated [including two Samaritan houses of prayer], six attested and five disputed). This adds to the evidence supporting the hypothesis that the synagogue, as a single-purpose building for Jewish worship, did not really develop until after the destruction of Jerusalem and the expulsion of the Jews from the city following the Second Revolt against Rome (132–135). As has been already noted, the center of Judaism shifted from Judea to Galilee after the disastrous Second Revolt led by Bar Kochba.

Of course, the center of Judea was Jerusalem. The Babylonian Talmud gives the number of synagogues in Jerusalem at the time of the First Revolt (66–70) as 394 (b Ket 105a), while the Jerusalem Talmud gives an even higher number: 480 (y Meg 3:1). Both refer to a synagogue built in the Temple area (y Sot 7:7-8; b Yom 7:1), but the existence of a synagogue there is highly doubtful.[1] Similarly, the details about first century Jerusalem given in the two Talmudim that are products of the sixth century are not always accurate in their descriptions of earlier periods. In any case, it is certainly possible that a great number of these "synagogues" were indistinguishable from domestic architecture. Suffice it to say that no validated synagogue from Jerusalem has, as yet, been discovered. The only archaeological evidence of the existence of a synagogue in Jerusalem is the Theodotus inscription that has been discussed earlier.

---

[1] Sidney B. Hoenig, "The Supposititious Temple-Synagogue," *Jewish Quarterly Review* 54/2 (1963) 115–31. Reprinted in Gutmann 1975, 55–71.

In 1949, the building housing David's tomb and the Cenacle just outside Jerusalem's Old City was inspected for damage.[2] In the course of the inspection, the three walls remaining from the original building were dated to the late Roman period. The western wall of the building dates from the Mameluke period while the cenotaph of David is from the Crusader period. The walls were made of plaster and traces of Greek letters have been found on some plaster fragments. The original floor may have been stone or mosaic set in plaster; only the plaster survived. Above this is a mosaic floor with geometric patterns. The floor that abuts the cenotaph is plaster. Bellarmino Bagatti, O.F.M., suggests that this building was a cult center for "Judeo-Christians" since the Cenacle is the traditional Christian site of the Last Supper.[3] There is insufficient evidence to determine what the building's function was or who built it. Its identification as a synagogue is disputed. There are some who make this identification, but the building lacks inscriptions or Jewish symbols to make that identification probable.

Twelve miles south of Jerusalem is the Herodion, a monumental structure built by Herod the Great some time after 40 B.C.E. to serve as a fortress, administrative center, and his mausoleum (see illust. 10).[4] It was one of the last holdouts against the Romans in the First Revolt and served as a command post for the rebels in the Second Revolt. In its final phase of occupation, the site served as a monastery between the fifth and sixth centuries. It was excavated by Virgilio Corbo, O.F.M., between 1962 and 1967. Following the 1967 war, Gideon Foerster, an Israeli archaeologist, took over the excavations. Recently, Ehud Netzer from Hebrew University has been excavating below the fortress.

One of the rooms inside Herod's fortress has been identified as a triclinium (an elaborate dining room), though it may have been a simple assembly hall. During the First Revolt, this room was altered. Corbo notes the addition of benches,[5] while Foerster maintains that four columns resting on a stylobate were also added. These architectural features were enough to convince Foerster that the Zealots turned Herod's triclinium into a synagogue.[6] The principal entrance to the

---

[2] J. Pinkerfled, "David's Tomb: Notes on the History of the Building, Preliminary Report," *Rabinowitz Bulletin* 3 (December 1960) 41–43.

[3] Bellarmino Bagatti, O.F.M., *The Church from the Gentiles in Palestine* (Jerusalem: Franciscan Press, 1973) 25.

[4] No tomb has yet been found. Josephus' accounts of Herod's funeral are not in agreement (*Antiquities* 17:199 and *War* 1:673).

[5] Virgilio Corbo, O.F.M., "L'Herodion de Gebal Fueridis," *Liber Annuus* 17 (1967) 101–03.

[6] Gideon Foerster, "The Synagogues of Masada and Herodium," in Levine 1982, 24–29.

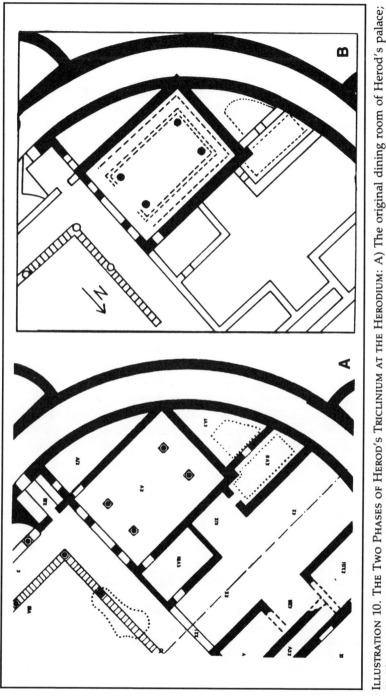

ILLUSTRATION 10. THE TWO PHASES OF HEROD'S TRICLINIUM AT THE HERODIUM: A) The original dining room of Herod's palace; B) The putative synagogue of the First Revolt. The addition of benches around three sides of the room convinced some that Herod's triclinium became the Zealot's synagogue.

room faces east and contributes to its identification as a synagogue based on a disputed Talmudic ruling which states that the entrance to a synagogue must face the east in order to imitate the orientation of the Temple (b Meg. 4:22). While the room Herod built was indeed altered by the Zealots, there is no real proof that they did so to transform it into a synagogue. There are no inscriptions to that effect nor are there any Jewish religious symbols in evidence.

The very question of the existence of synagogues as early as the first century is still not settled.[7] Other sites in Judah that have been identified as having ancient synagogues without conclusive evidence are Horvat Karmil, Horvat Midras, and Khirbet 'Aziz.[8] There are some synagogues in Judea whose existence is attested by the presence of architectural or decorative fragments having Jewish inscriptions, but the locations of the structures themselves are unknown. These include the Jerusalem synagogue of the Theodotus inscription, Kefar Bilu, Na'aneh, Emmaus (Nicopolis), Beth Guvrin, and Horvat Kishor.[9]

Two Samaritan Synagogues

Of the remaining synagogues of Judea, two were probably used by Samaritans rather than Jews.[10] One is located at Salbit, a town on the Jerusalem-to-Ramleh highway. During the fourth century C.E., the Samaritans experienced a revival under the leadership of Baba Rabbah. This "synagogue" may attest to that revival in Judea. The building is oriented to the northeast in the direction of Mount Gerizim, the mountain that was holy to the Samaritans (see John 4). There are three inscriptions in the Samaritan dialect of Hebrew—one of which reads, "The Lord shall reign for ever and ever." Another is the Samaritan recension of Exodus 15:18, and the third is fragmentary. There is also a two-line Greek inscription that is too fragmentary to decipher. It does, however, contain the word *eukterion*, that occurs frequently in Christian inscriptions which refer to renovated buildings. This has led to the suggestion that the building was restored by Samaritan Christians and was a church—not a Samaritan synagogue.[11]

---

[7] Marilyn Chiat, "First Century Synagogues: Methodological Problems," in Gutmann 1981, 49–60.

[8] For a description of these sites and relevant bibliography, see Chiat 1982, 238–39.

[9] See Chiat 1982, 201–02, 211–13, 218, 235–38.

[10] Ibid., 209–11, 215–17.

[11] R. Plummer, "New Evidence for Samaritan Christianity," *Catholic Biblical Quarterly* 41/1 (1979) 112–17.

A fifth century building in Huldah, 8.5 kilometers southwest of Rehovot, also may be a Samaritan synagogue because of its northward orientation.[12] Its mosaic floor contains typical Jewish symbols: the menorah, incense shovel, shofar, the lulab, and ethrog. A Greek inscription contains the phrase "good luck" that is unusual in Jewish inscriptions. The structure is rectangular and is composed of two rooms, one of which has two pools that probably were used for ritual immersions. That this structure was a place of worship seems to be certain; whether it was used by Jews or Samaritans is not so clear.

The Synagogue at 'En Gedi

There are some structures located in Judea that have been identified, with some certainty, as synagogues. One of these is located at the oasis at 'En Gedi on the western shore of the Dead Sea at a site occupied continuously from the seventh century B.C.E. until the sixth century C.E. During the middle Roman period (70–200 C.E.), a simple, irregularly-shaped rectangular hall was modified by the addition of pillars, benches, a narthex, and a chair of Moses. Also, the central door in the north wall of the building was blocked and transformed into a niche, thus orienting the building to Jerusalem. The floor of the synagogue was a simple white mosaic pavement with some black trim. At the south end of the floor, a black swastika in mosaic served as the floor's single decorative element. Clearly, the building was transformed into a synagogue.[13] In the Byzantine period the synagogue was remodeled again. A new mosaic floor was laid atop the old one. This time it was made of multicolored tesserae. Its design was a combination of geometric and floral designs with birds in the center and in each corner of the floor. A bema was placed in front of the niche. In the southwestern corner of the narthex, there was a *kiyor*, a basin used for washing prior to prayer. Though such basins are mentioned in rabbinic sources, this is the first one found in an ancient synagogue.[14]

The most interesting feature of the Byzantine period synagogue is its eighteen-line Aramaic and Hebrew inscription located in the western aisle. The Hebrew section of the inscription contains the text of 1 Chronicles 1:1-4, the names of the twelve signs of the zodiac and

[12] F. Hüttenmeister and G. Reeg, *Die Antiken Synagogen in Israel* 2 (Weisbaden: Reichert, 1977) 602.

[13] Dan Barag, "En-Gedi: The Synagogue," *Encyclopedia of Archaeological Excavations in the Holy Land* 2 ed. M. Avi-Yonah (Englewood Cliffs, N.J.: Prentice-Hall, 1976) 378–80; Dan Barag, Y. Porat, and Ehud Netzer, "The Synagogue at 'En-Gedi," in Levine 1982, 116–19; Chiat 1982, 219–24.

[14] Barag, Porat, and Netzer, "The Synagogue at 'En-Gedi," 117.

the twelve months of the year, the names of Abraham, Isaac, and Jacob, and the three companions of Daniel (Hanaiah, Mishael, and Azariah). It ends with "Peace upon Israel." While this inscription contained the names of the signs of the zodiac, it did not contain any representations of the zodiac as other synagogues did. Perhaps this gives some indication of the community's more conservative bent. The Aramaic section of the inscription curses those who cause dissension within the community, betray the secrets of the town,[15] or spread malicious gossip to the Gentiles. The next section of the inscription commemorates the laying of the mosaic. The remainder of the mosaic is illegible. One literary reference to this site comes from Eusebius, the fourth century Church historian, who characterized 'En Gedi as a very large Jewish village. The excavation of that city's synagogue has underscored the Jewish character of 'En Gedi and has given some idea of the relative wealth and religious sensibilities of its people.

The Synagogue at Eshtemoa

Another Judean synagogue also shows the conservative bent of the Jews of that region. The synagogue of Eshtemoa was decorated without any of the human or animal images used in some synagogues of Galilee. The floor of the synagogue was decorated with a mosaic of floral and geometric patterns. A number of architectural fragments contain reliefs, but these likewise have floral and geometric patterns, though some have menorahs.[16] In fact, it was the discovery of architectural fragments with embossed menorahs built into the houses of the modern Arab village of as-Samu that led to the survey of the site and the discovery of the synagogue.

The Arabic name of the village probably is related to the ancient Hebrew name of the site that is located fifteen kilometers south of Hebron. The Bible mentions an Eshtemoa (Josh 15:50; 1 Sam 30:28, and 1 Chr 6:42). The synagogue of the village was built at the end of the Roman period and was remodeled in the Byzantine period. The synagogue is a broadhouse measuring 13.33 by 21.30 meters with two-tiered benches along the northern and southern walls. It has a triple entrance way in the eastern wall that opens to a small narthex. Though the only entrance to the building is on the east, the orientation of the synagogue is toward the north (in the direction of Jerusalem). The eastern entrance may reflect the belief of some rabbis that synagogue en-

---

[15] These secrets may have had something to do with the cultivation and processing of balsam for which the village was famous.

[16] Chait 1982, 227.

trances were to duplicate the eastern entrance of the Temple (see b. Meg 4:22). The three niches in the northern wall, as well as the stone double-tiered bema below them, show that the prayers were said facing Jerusalem. An Aramaic inscription which is not fully preserved identifies the patrons of the synagogue.[17] The building was converted into a mosque in the seventh century. A *mihrab*, a Muslim prayer niche, was cut into the benches along the southern wall in accordance with the tradition of directing prayers towards Mecca. Probably the absence of representational art in the synagogue facilitated its conversion into a mosque.

The Synagogue at Horvat Rimmon

Fitting into this regional pattern of conservativism regrading representational art is the synagogue of Horvat Rimmon, located near Kibbutz Lahav some ten kilometers south of Hebron. The synagogue, located in what was an important regional commercial center in the Roman and Byzantine periods reveals that no animal or human figures adorned the structure, though many decorative architectural fragments were found at the site.[18] The synagogue itself was basilical in form with a northern orientation, though its triple facade was in the southern wall. A northern orientation is presumed because of remnants of what may have been a bema along the north wall. What was unique about this synagogue is that the entire building was surrounded by an enclosure wall erected at the end of the sixth century.

The Synagogue at Khirbet Susiya

The only other ancient synagogue to have been uncovered in Judea was found at Khirbet Susiya, a site which was not mentioned in any ancient text. Though it was described by a British survey team in the last century, it was not systematically excavated until 1971–72 in a project directed by S. Gutman, Z. Yeivin, and Ehud Netzer on behalf of the Israeli Department of Antiquities.[19] The synagogue was built at the end of the fourth century and was in use continuously until the ninth century. At that time, it fell into disuse until the tenth century when its courtyard was converted into a mosque.

[17] Z. Yeivin, ''The Synagogue of Eshtemoa,'' in Levine 1982, 122.

[18] Amos Kloner, ''Hurvat Rimmon, 1979,'' *Israel Exploration Journal* 30 (1980) 226–28.

[19] Gutmann, Yeivan, and Netzer, ''Excavations in the Synagogue at Horvat Susiya,'' in Levine 1982, 123–28.

The plan of the building remained the same throughout the five centuries of its use. It is a large broadhouse—nine by sixteen meters—constructed with skillfully cut ashlars. Its triple doorway façade faces the east. Its northern orientation is obvious from the elaborate bema and a niche located in the center of the northern wall. A secondary bema is located in the eastern section of the building. There once were benches located along the southern and western walls and a portion of the northern wall as well. Unlike the other synagogues in Judea, this one had a gallery. It was a later addition to the building since the western wall of the structure had to be reinforced. East of the synagogue was a open courtyard surrounded on three sides by a roofed portico. Its western side opened to the synagogue's narthex. The floor of the narthex was composed of a colored mosaics set in an interlaced pattern.

The floor of the synagogue itself is made up of three mosaic panels. The eastern most panel depicts a Torah shrine, two menorahs, a lulab, and an ethrog with columns on either side. Next to the columns is a landscape with deer and rams. The center panel is composed of geometric and floral patterns. Directly in front of the central bema is what looks like a spoked wheel, though Gutman believes it to be the remnants of a zodiac wheel.[20] The west panel is severely damaged. Its subject is uncertain though it has been suggested that it depicts Daniel in the lion's den.[21] The unique feature of this synagogue is the number of inscriptions it contains. There are four inscriptions in the mosaics and nineteen fragmentary inscriptions etched into the marble of the building.[22] These Hebrew and Aramaic inscriptions name the donors and patrons of this well endowed synagogue.

Conclusion

The synagogues of Judea illustrate the diversity there is in synagogue art and architecture, though the decorative schemes of these buildings reflect a conservative attitude toward representational art. This conservativism is likely a characteristic of the Jews of this region. That only six Jewish synagogues have been identified in Judea probably reflects a shift in Jewish population from Judah to Galilee in the

[20] Gutmann, Yeivan, and Netzer, "Excavations at Horvat Susiya," Levine 1982, 126.

[21] Chiat 1982, 233.

[22] S. Gutmann, "Excavations in the Synagogue at Horvat Susiya," and Z. Yeivin, "Inscribed Marble Fragments from the Khirbet Susiya Synagogue," *Israel Exploration Journal* 24 (1974) 126-28, 201-09.

second and third centuries. In Galilee three times as many ancient synagogues have been discovered. Finally, excavations have uncovered no undisputed synagogue from before the second century in Judea. That single-purpose buildings intended for Jewish worship existed before that time seems unlikely.

Chapter 4

The Zodiac Synagogues

Introduction

There are four ancient synagogues in Palestine that have what initially appears to be quite an unusual decorative motif: a mosaic of the zodiac on their floors. Even though some Jewish communities were more liberal than others with regard to representational art in the synagogue, the use of the zodiac seems to be out of place, not only because of the biblical injunction against images (Exod 20:4; Deut 5:8), but also because of the prohibition of divination (Deut 18:9-14). There is some textual evidence that astrological ideas were assimilated by the Jews despite these biblical injunctions. Zodiacal documents have been found among the Dead Sea Scrolls. One zodiac from Qumran's cave four is known to exist (4Q Zodiac) but it has not yet been published.[1] In addition, there is an encoded series of horoscopes in which three people are described with reference to their astrological signs.[2] Evidently, the people of Qumran had no problem integrating astrology with their Judaism even though they are considered to have been a most conservative group. The Mishnah, Talmud, and other rabbinic sources indicate a positive view towards astrology. For example, the Babylonian Talmud tells the story of Rabbi Joseph bar Hiyya who turned down the opportunity to preside over a rabbinic academy in Babylon because astrologers predicted that his term would last but two

---

[1] Michael Wise, "The Dead Sea Scrolls," pt. 2, *Biblical Archaeologist* 49/4 (1986) 238.

[2] For more information about the astrology at Qumran, see M. Delcor, "Recherces sur un horoscope en langue hebräique provenant de Qumran," *Revue de Qumran* 5 (1966) 521–42; and Robert Gordis, "A Document in Code from Qumran—Some Observations," *Journal of Semitic Studies* 11 (1966) 37–39. Some Qumran astrological texts have been published by J. T. Milik. See his *The Books of Enoch: Aramaic Fragments of Qumran Cave 4* (Oxford: Clarendon, 1976) 7–22, 273–97.

years (b Berakoth 64a). One reason for the influence of astrology in Judaism was due to geography. Babylon, the major Jewish intellectual center outside of Palestine, had a long astrological tradition. Such influence was felt in Palestine as well since there was a considerable flow of communication between the rabbis of Palestine and Babylon.[3] The nonpolemical references to astrology among rabbinic texts shows that some rabbis did not consider astrology incompatible with Judaism. The texts from Qumran and the rabbis, plus the archaeological data, show that astrological interest was more pervasive and acceptable than has been realized. The Qumran material represents the views of a Jewish group which flourished between 150 B.C.E. and 70 C.E. The synagogues with the zodiac mosaics show that interest in astrology among some Jews continued into the Byzantine period.

The four synagogues are rather widely distributed geographically. Beth Alpha is located in the eastern part of the Jezreel Valley at the foot of Mount Gilboa. Ḥamat Tiberias is located on the western shore of the Sea of Galilee about 1.5 kilometers south of the modern city of Tiberias. Ḥusifah on Mount Carmel overlooks the Kishon River thirteen kilometers southeast of Haifa. Na'aran is located at an oasis 5.5 kilometers northwest of Jericho. The excavators of the synagogue of Khirbet Susiya assert that a zodiac decorated the floor of that synagogue but the mosaic is really too fragmentary to be certain.[4] Finally, the synagogue of 'En Gedi has an inscription of the names of the zodiac signs but no depiction of the zodiac itself. This chapter will consider the four synagogues whose zodiac mosaic is obvious.

In each occurrence of the zodiac in a Palestinian synagogue, the design is the same: there are two concentric circles inscribed within a square. The central circle depicts the Greek god of the sun, Helios, riding on a chariot with the moon and the stars in the background. The outer circle is divided into twelve segments—one for each of the signs of the zodiac. The corners of the squares are decorated with female figures representing the four seasons. The design is balanced and uniform. This suggests that all four mosaics are derived from some common prototype.[5] This, in turn, may suggest that the zodiac had more than an aesthetic function.

[3] James F. Strange, "Archaeology and the Religion of Judaism in Palestine," *Aufstieg und Niedergang der Römischen Welt* II.19.1, 670–71.

[4] S. Gutmann, Z. Yeivan, and E. Netzer, "Excavation in the Synagogue at Horvat Susiya," Levine 1982, 126.

[5] Similar designs found elsewhere in the Roman world show no such harmony in terms of form and content. See Rachel Hachlili, "The Zodiac in Ancient Jewish Art: Representation and Significance," *Bulletin of the American Schools of Oriental Research* 228 (1977) 61–62.

The Synagogue at Beth Alpha

Beth Alpha is one of six verified synagogues in the region surrounding Beth She'an whose Hellenistic name was Scythopolis, one the cities of the Decapolis. Scythopolis was founded by Greeks during the Ptolemaic period, so the evidence of Hellenistic influence is not very surprising here. In fact, of the region's six synagogues, four (Beth Alpha, Beth She'an B, Tel Menora, and Ma'oz Hayyim) have figurative motifs, though all six (which include, besides the four above, Beth She'an A and Rehov) are decorated with the more traditional menorah.

The Beth Alpha synagogue was originally built in the fifth century; however, the mosaic floor with the zodiac was added in the sixth century.[6] The building was an apsidal basilica (see illust. 11). The apse that was against the southern wall oriented the building to Jerusalem. In the floor of the apse is a hole covered by a paver which could have served to store valuables of the community.

The zodiac is the centerpiece of a three-panel mosaic floor that was designed in a primitive style. The panel below the zodiac depicts the binding of Isaac (Gen 22:1-19). The scene includes details not found in the Bible but in the Targum. Above the zodiac is a panel showing a Torah shrine, two large menorahs, an incense shovel, the lulab, and ethrog.

The central panel contains the zodiac. In the middle of the zodiac is Helios with his chariot against the night sky. The signs of the zodiac are portrayed in a wheel. The twelve signs start at three o'clock and run counterclockwise. Female personifications of the four seasons are found at the four corners of the panels but not in places that correspond to the appropriate zodiac signs. Two of the signs are presented in a nontraditional form. Usually, Saggitarius is a centaur; here, it is portrayed in human form. Aquarius is normally portrayed drawing water. Here, the figure is pouring water from an amphora.

Jerome Murphy-O'Connor makes the ingenious suggestion that the placement of the zodiac between the two religious panels reduces it to a merely decorative role.[7] The story of the binding of Isaac is an implicit condemnation of astrology since it demonstrates that the future is in God's hands. Similarly, the Torah shrine on the topmost panel intimates that the future of the worshippers is determined by their obedience to the Torah.

---

[6] The mosaic includes an inscription that provides a date during the "reign of Justin" who may be either Justinian I (518–27) or Justinian II (565–78). The inscription is in Aramaic and is broken off at the point where the date was given.

[7] Murphy-O'Connor 1986, 161.

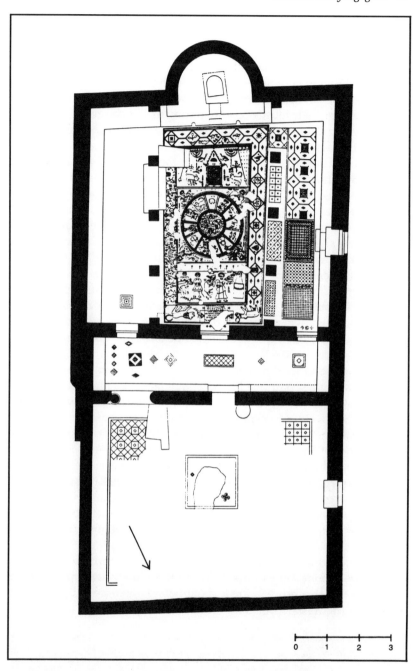

ILLUSTRATION 11. THE PLAN OF THE BETH ALPHA SYNAGOGUE.
Note the zodiac, the apse, and the narthex.

The Synagogue at Ḥamat Tiberias

The zodiac is also the centerpiece of another three-panel mosaic in the synagogue of Ḥamat Tiberias.[8] This structure was a first-century public building until it was converted in the third century to be used exclusively for Jewish worship. The zodiac mosaic was added in the fourth century. This fourth-century dating makes the zodiac the oldest found in Palestine. The building was remodeled in the fifth century and the mosaic was covered over.

The building with the zodiac floor was a broadhouse measuring thirteen by fifteen meters and was divided into four areas by three rows of columns (see illust. 12). The area between the two eastern most rows of columns served as the nave since it was the widest space. There was a triple entrance way in the northern wall. At the southern end of the nave, there was an entrance into a raised room which was apparently the permanent location of the Torah shrine. East of the nave the floor was decorated with a multicolored mosaic with geometric patterns. From fragments discovered in the debris, it appears that the inner walls of the building were adorned with colored frescoes.

The floor of the nave was decorated with a mosaic made up of three panels. The southernmost panel (the one closest to the Torah shrine) depicted a Torah shrine flanked by a menorah on each side. Surrounding the menorahs are the lulab, shofar, ethrog, and an incense shovel. The Torah shrine is portrayed as a rectangular cabinet topped by gabled roof with a conch shell. A curtain knotted in the middle hangs in front of the shrine's closed doors.

The middle panel contains the zodiac with Helios riding his chariot in the center.[9] The twelve signs run counterclockwise each taking a segment of the circle that surrounds Helios. At the corners of the panel are the busts of four female figures representing the four seasons with their names given in Hebrew. Two features of the zodiac indicate that its artist was probably not Jewish. The nude figure of Libra is shown uncircumcised, and the word *deli* (Aquarius) is written in mirror-image reverse.

The third panel contains a lengthy Greek inscription flanked by two lions. Divided into nine squares, the panel contains names of donors. One of these, Severus, must have been especially generous since two squares are devoted to him. Inscriptions in the eastern aisle

[8] For a complete presentation on the synagogue see Moshe Dothan, *Hamath Tiberias—Early Synagogues and the Hellenistic and Roman Remains.* (Jerusalem: Israel Department of Antiquities, 1983).

[9] The construction of a wall for the fifth-century synagogue obliterated the chariot.

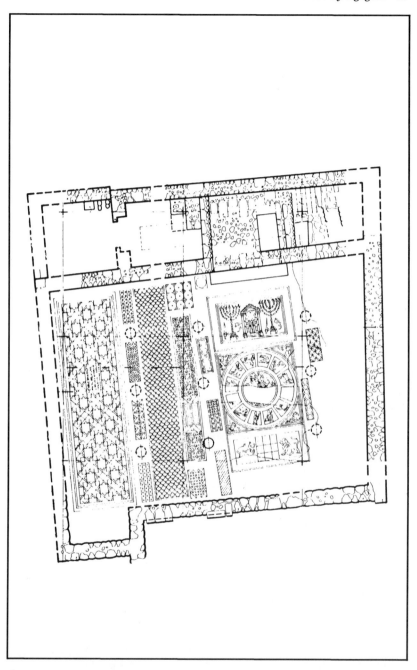

ILLUSTRATION 12. THE PLAN OF THE SYNAGOGUE AT ḤAMAT TIBERIAS WITH ITS ZODIAC FLOOR.

also mention Severus. This area also contains another Greek inscription and one in Aramaic; both refer to donors.

The Synagogue at Ḥusifah

This village located on Mount Carmel, overlooking the Kishon River, is located about thirteen kilometers southeast of Haifa. Its synagogue was built at the highest point in the village, following a usual custom. A firm date for the synagogue has not been established. The excavators suggest a sixth-century date because of its similarity to the Beth Alpha synagogue.[10] The building was almost square (10.1 by 10.7 meters) and was divided into a central nave and two side aisles by two rows of columns with five columns per row. The orientation of the synagogue is in doubt. Both an eastward and southward orientation have been suggested.[11]

The floor of the synagogue is adorned with tesserae of various shades of limestone, blue marble chips and green glass fragments. Along the wall, the designs in the mosaic are geometrical, though along the western side the mosaic depicts traditional Jewish symbols: the menorah, shofar, lulab, ethrog, and incense shovel. A wreath frames a Hebrew inscription that reads: "Peace upon Israel." The mosaic in the center of the nave is decorated with floral designs as well as portraits of various birds. Its centerpiece is a zodiac preserved in a fragmentary state. Of the twelve signs only the five from Saggitarius to Aries remain. Similarly, just one corner of the mosaic survived and it depicts a woman's head which is encircled by pomegranates, dates and a sickle. Though this appears to be a personification of autumn, the head is placed next to the spring months.[12] The damaged state of the mosaic is not due to defacing by iconoclasts but to the fire that destroyed the building.

The Synagogue at Na'aran

This site is located at an oasis about 5.5 kilometers northwest of Jericho. It is mentioned by Eusebius (*Onomasticon* 136:24) as a large Jewish village. The ancient synagogue's mosaic floor was discovered as a result of bombing that occurred during a skirmish between British and Ottoman forces in 1918. It was excavated in the 1920s by L. J. Vin-

---

[10] Michael Avi-Yonah and N. Makhouly, "A Sixth-Century Synagogue at 'Isfiya," *Quarterly of the Department of Antiquities in Palestine* 3 (1933) 118–31.

[11] Chiat 1982, 159.

[12] A similar dislocation occurs at Beth Alpha.

cent of the École Biblique, though a final report was not published until 1961. The synagogue was part of a larger architectural complex that included courts and annexes all of which were surrounded by a wall.

The synagogue was a basilica (21 by 14.8 meters) oriented toward Jerusalem to the south with its main entrance on the north. Directly in front of the main entrance is a rectangular panel that frames an ornate and highly stylized menorah. The panel is flanked by Aramaic inscriptions that name benefactors of the synagogue.

The floor of the nave has a mosaic divided into three panels. The first panel is decorated with geometric, floral and faunal figures. Many of the animal figures have been mutilated. The second panel contains the zodiac, the figures which likewise have been effaced, though the names of the signs remain (see illust. 13). In the center of the zodiac is Helios driving his chariot. Framing the zodiac are depictions of the four seasons. The figures of Helios and the four seasons are almost completely removed. The third panel has also been defaced because

ILLUSTRATION 13. AN ARTIST'S RENDERING OF WHAT REMAINS OF THE ZODIAC AT NA'ARAN.

it contains the picture of a man in the posture of prayer.[13] The name, "Daniel," is inscribed to the right of this figure leading some to suggest that the panel depicted Daniel in the lions' den.[14]

A second scene in this panel has the more traditional Jewish symbols: a Torah shrine flanked by two menorahs. Ten inscriptions naming benefactors of the synagogue were set in the mosaic floor as well. The dating of the mosaic floor has been a problem.[15] Vincent first dated the floor to the first century A.D. on the basis of the mosaic's style though he revised the date to the third century. Recently, dates in the fifth and sixth centuries have been suggested.

Conclusion

The most common explanation of the presence of pagan zodiac mosaics in Jewish synagogues is that they are simply artistic motifs without any specific astrological connections.[16] But such an explanation ignores the written sources that contain positive references to astrology. Some explain the apparent disregard of the second commandment by asserting that these floors were laid when idolatry was no longer a problem for the Jews. It is obvious, however, that not all Jewish communities were so liberal in their interpretation of the prohibition of images. In fact, the zodiac at Na'aran was defaced by Jewish iconoclasts who were apparently offended by the human and animal figures.

Rachel Hachlili, developing a suggestion of Michael Avi-Yonah, asserts that the zodiac panels in these four synagogues were not merely aesthetic but also functional. The zodiac served as a calendar reminding worshippers of the annual rituals celebrated by the community.[17] The presence of zodiacs in all four synagogues shows an attempt to unify the zodiac and the agricultural calendar, the latter being rep-

---

[13] The destruction of the animal and human figures depicted in this mosaic shows that there were some Jews who were deeply offended by the representation of living creatures. That the defacing of this mosaic was done by Jews seems to be indicated by the careful preservation of the Hebrew words in the course of destroying the images.

[14] Michael Avi-Yonah, "Na'aran," *Encyclopedia of Archaeological Excavations in the Holy Land* 3:891-94.

[15] L. H. Vincent, "Le Sanctuarie Juif d''Ain Doug," *Revue biblique* 28 (1919) 532–63; and his "Un Sanctuarie dans la Region de Jericho, La Synagogue de Na'arah," *Revue biblique* 65 (1961) 163–73; Chiat 1982, 260.

[16] See E. R. Goodenough, *Jewish Symbols in the Greco-Roman World* (New York: Pantheon, 1958) 8:215.

[17] Hachlili, "The Zodiac in Ancient Jewish Art," 73–76.

resented by the four seasons. The result is a liturgical calendar for the synagogue. The annual rituals that the priests formerly performed in the Temple now had to be carried on by the community in its synagogue. That is why the zodiac is given such a central place in the synagogue despite its association with astrology and the use of representational art.

This explanation, though plausible, is not entirely satisfactory. A fixed calendar was not introduced until about 325 C.E. (probably after the Tiberias floor was laid, though before the other floors were laid); and if the zodiac was a calendar, why is it that the seasons and the signs are coordinated nowhere except at the Tiberias synagogue? Second, presumably the zodiac would have been aligned with the Roman solar calendar, which could not have been properly reconciled with the Jewish lunar calendar. Finally, the zodiac could not have been used as a calendar—at least in the modern sense of the word.

If the zodiac did not function as a calendar, what was it doing in the synagogues? The probable explanation lies with the obvious: some Jews believed in the superstition behind astrology. It has been suggested that some Palestinian Jews of the Byzantine period considered Helios to be a kind of "super-angel" who had the power to affect people's lives.[18] The belief that the planets influence people's lives was part of the cultural baggage of the day.[19] Then, as now, some believers saw no conflict between traditional beliefs and astrology. Still, no explanation of the presence of the zodiac in early Jewish synagogues has been able to win significant support. Their presence in these synagogues remains an enigma.

[18] Levine 1982, 9.
[19] Ephesians 6:12 and Colossians 1:16 may be evidence of similar beliefs.

Chapter 5

The Church: Preliminary Issues

Introduction

While the origins of the synagogue is still a debated issue, and the dating of a number of ancient synagogues in Palestine is still not firmly established, the beginnings of Christian architecture are not so mysterious. First, we know where and when the first church buildings would have appeared. From the very beginning, a central feature of the Christian faith was the assembly of believers. At first, the Christians of Palestine continued to worship in the Temple (Acts 3:1) and in local synagogues as long as they were allowed. Jews who believed that Jesus of Nazareth was the Messiah eventually had to find their own places to worship.[1] No doubt they continued to follow the practices of the Jews and met in private homes, city squares, markets, and rented rooms. The early communities did not have the economic resources, the organizational structure, or even the need to develop a distinctive Christian architecture. They met where convenient. But from the beginning, a distinctive liturgy developed that required regular gatherings. Because of the nature of these gatherings, they were held in the homes of believers. The core of the service was a meal and, consequently, the place of meeting needed to be able to accommodate a number of people for "dinner": "And day by day, attending the temple together and breaking bread in their homes, they partook of food with glad and generous hearts." (Acts 2:46).

Christians, then, met in each others homes. In time, some of these homes were renovated to serve exclusively as places of worship. These are the *domus ecclesiae*—the house churches. These house churches were indistinguishable from any other house in the neighborhood. Certainly the first Christians did not want to call attention to themselves since

---

[1] John 9:22, 34 probably reflect the decision of Jewish religious authorities to expel those who professed Jesus as the Messiah from their religious communities.

the attention might bring hostility. One example of such a structure is the church at Dura-Europos. What was once a private home in this Syrian city became a Christian meeting place sometime before the middle of the third century.[2] This also occurred in Galilee with the "House of Peter" located in Capernaum.[3] Prior to the time of Constantine it seems that Christian congregations worshipped in private homes or in specially venerated caves.[4]

Archaeologists, by means of surveys and full scale excavations, have done a remarkably complete job of contributing to our understanding of the beginnings of ecclesiastical architecture. Some 276 structures in Palestine have been excavated and identified as churches, a remarkable number. This is more than five times the number of synagogues discovered in Palestine—including disputed synagogues. The data base provided by the remains of these ancient churches provides invaluable information about the early Church in Palestine. The excavation of these church structures has disclosed the beliefs, liturgy, piety, social standing, and the economic—political status of the Christians in Palestine during the first centuries of the Church's life.

Most of the churches in Palestine were built to serve the liturgical needs of local Christian communities. Of course, other motives entered into the decision to erect particular churches. Some churches were built in memory of a particular person, usually a saint named in an inscription within the church. About forty-five such churches have survived. These are called "dedicated churches." Another type is the "memorial church": churches built at the site where, according to local tradition, a particular event in the life of Jesus occurred. Besides the Church of the Holy Sepulchre in Jerusalem, and the Church of the Nativity in Bethlehem, other examples of "memorial churches" include the Church of the Annunciation in Nazareth, the Church of the Ascension in Jerusalem, and the Mensa Christi on the northwestern shore of the Sea of Galilee. In all, about twenty such memorial churches have been identified. Finally, about forty-five percent of the churches of

---

[2] A complete treatment of this building is given in Carl H. Kraeling, *The Christian Building. Excavations at Dura-Europos* (Locust Valley, N.Y.: J. J. Augustin, 1967). A short, popular treatment is given in Graydon F. Snyder, *Ante Pacem* (Macon, Ga.: Mercer Press, 1985) 68–71. See Richard Krautheimer, *Early Christian and Byzantine Architecture* (Baltimore, Md.: Penguin Books, rev. ed. 1975) 24–34, for a review of other such structures outside Palestine.

[3] The "house of Peter" will be discussed in chapter six. Synder does not believe that this structure can be identified as a *domus ecclesiae* though he gives no reason for his hesitancy. See his *Ante Pacem*, 67–68, 72.

[4] For a discussion of caves as places of Christian worship see Bagatti 1971, 112–36.

Palestine were part of a larger architectural complex. Some chapels were part of monastic settlements, others were located in cemeteries. Some churches served as fortresses and others were parts of guest-houses.

The Beginnings of Church Architecture in Palestine

As was the case with synagogues, the earliest churches in Palestine were not distinguishable from domestic architecture. In fact, the first Christian assemblies apparently gathered in private homes—called *domus ecclesiae* (house churches).[5] According to Eusebius a large church stood in Jerusalem already before the Second Revolt (135 c.e.), though by Eusebius' lifetime the revolt was just a memory.[6] Eusebius states that a construction spurt occurred during the interval of peace between the reign of Gallienus (260–268) and the beginning of Diocletian's (284–305) persecution, when large churches were founded in almost every town in Palestine.[7]

Many churches went up following Constantine's Edict of Milan (313) which made Christianity the religion of the empire. The emperor encouraged the building of churches in Galilee in order to help Christianity achieve inroads into the Jewish population of that region. Constantine chose Joseph of Tiberias, a converted Jew, to carry out this project. St. Epiphanius indicates that Joseph built churches in Sepphoris, Nazareth, Tiberias, and Capernaum.[8] Joseph's work, however, did not have its intended effect, for he was not able to attract Jewish converts to Christianity. During the Constantinian period, the Church of the Resurrection (*Anastasis*) and the Eleona Church were built in Jerusalem, and the Church of the Nativity in Bethlehem.

There was a spate of building activity at this time. Monasteries and hospices for pilgrims were built. The Byzantines enforced Hadrian's ban on the presence of Jews in Jerusalem. The only day the Byzantines allowed Jews in Jersualem was on the ninth day of the Hebrew month of Av when Jews mourned the destruction of the Temple.

The next great period of church building in Palestine took place as a result of the activity of the empress Eudocia, the estranged wife of Theodosius II (401–460). She built churches in Jerusalem and its environs. These were small edifices. Among the churches the empress

---

[5] For more information on house churches see Lloyd Michael White, *Domus Ecclesiae—Domus Dei* (unpublished Ph.D. dissertation, Yale University, 1982).

[6] *Demonstratio evangelica*, 3, 5, 108.

[7] *Historia ecclesiae*, 8, 1.

[8] J. P. Migne, *Patrologiae cursus completus series graeca.* (Paris: J. P. Migne, 1863) 41: para. 410–11.

is responsible for are the Church of Saint Stephen in Jerusalem. It was destroyed in 614 by the Persians along with the other churches of the city. Eudocia also interceded for the Jews so they could once again live in Jerusalem.

The last great period of church building in Palestine occurred during the reign of Justinian I (527–563). The building activity of this period was the result of the economic prosperity and political stability that marked the almost forty-year reign of Justinian. Sixty-nine churches have been dated to Justinian's reign. The Church of the Nativity in Bethlehem with its elaborate ornamentation shows the extent of the financial support the emperor gave to the construction of churches in Palestine. Most of the churches whose ruins have survived were built during Justinian's reign.

After the great activity of the sixth century a decline in church building took place, particularly while the Persians ruled Palestine from 614 to 628. During this time many churches were destroyed. The decline in building activity during Persian rule was not confined to the construction of churches. The decline was quite general and was due to the political upheavals that came as a result of the military conquest in the first half of the seventh century. After the Byzantines succeeded in expelling the Persians, building activity was renewed.

This spurt of new activity, however, was short lived due to the Arab invasion of Palestine in the early part of the seventh century. After the Arab conquest of Palestine in 638, construction of churches ceased almost entirely. The few churches that were built during the early Arab period retained a Byzantine architectural style. For example, at Khirbet en-Nitla, three miles east of Jericho in the Jordan Valley, J. L. Kelso and D. C. Baramki excavated a church that showed five stages of construction, two of which came after the Arab conquest of Palestine.[9]

The Architectural Style of Church Buildings

As was the case with synagogue architecture, the architecture of early church buildings shows a transference of architectural forms from Greco-Roman civic buildings. Christians chose to avoid architectural forms associated with non-Christian worship.[10] The most common type of ecclesiastical construction in Palestine was the basilica. One hundred fifty-five of the churches in Palestine were built according to this

[9] Asher Ovadiah, *Corpus of the Byzantine Churches in the Holy Land* (Bonn: Peter Hanstein Verlag, 1970) 114–16.
[10] Yoram Tsafrir, "The Byzantine Setting and its Influence on Ancient Synagogues," in Levine 1987, 150.

pattern. One reason for the predominance of this form was the simplicity and ease of construction of basilicas. Since this type of building was quite common in Palestine, both architects and laborers were familiar with it. There were, however, some significant innovations introduced by Christian architects. For example, a few basilicas had a transept added. The addition of this new architectural feature gave new religious significance to the Greco-Roman basilica since it made the building cruciform. The cruciform plan did not exist in Roman architecture nor did it appear in synagogue architecture. This new style was probably the invention of Byzantine architects who wished to give symbolic meaning to the building by emphasizing the cross. This form also had the practical effect of allowing more worshippers to stand close to the altar.

Another innovation in the architecture of the Greco-Roman basilica involved a departure from the standard basilical plan with its central nave and two side aisles. There were a few important structures, such as the Church of the Holy Sepulchre in Jerusalem and the Church of the Nativity in Bethlehem, which were basilical in form but with five subdivisions: a central nave and two aisles at either side.

A second type of church building is the chapel. In its simplest form, the chapel is made up of a single hall with an apse. The church at Tabgha is a standard chapel. A development of this form involved attaching a triple apse in the form of a clover leaf to the hall. The apsidal transept was the result of this development. The triple apse has no practical function since all the liturgical actions are performed in the central part of the church. Its principal role is to create a cruciform effect. Ninety-three chapels have been excavated in Palestine.

The architectural category with the fewest number of representatives is the centralized church. Only seven churches of this category have been found in Palestine. There are two types of centralized churches: the octagonal and the circular. The church of Saint Peter in Capernaum is an example of the octagonal type while the church of the Ascension of the Mount of Olives is an example of the circular type. The centralized churches reveal the influence of the circular Roman mausoleums. They have the practical effect of drawing worshippers toward the altar.

Typical Features of Church Buildings

More than 130 churches in Palestine have an apse. Of these, about twenty have a triple apse. This popular feature of ecclesiastical architecture served to orient the building toward the east, the usual orientation for early churches. The development of the triple apse was a distinctive Christian innovation that transformed the church into a cruciform structure. On either side of the single apse many churches have two rooms known as the pastophoria. One of the rooms served as a robing room for the clergy. It was known as the diaconicon. The prothesis was the other room; it was used for the presentation and preparation of offerings. These rooms were in use until the sixth century when developments in the liturgy made them obsolete. The bema took up the east section of the church and was usually a few steps higher than the floor of the hall. It was the location of the altar and the schola cantorum.

The altar itself was a table resting on four legs. Sometimes the legs of the altar were set into sockets to stabilize it. Behind the altar was the synthronos which served as seating for the clergy, who were arranged in a semicircle around the apse. The bishop's seat was in the center of the synthronos and a little higher than the rest. Only a few churches show any trace of an ambo—usually on the base. Still, this reveals that the position of the ambo was in the northeast corner of the nave just in front of the bema.

About one-third of the churches excavated have a narthex. This structure had two purposes. For one thing, it served as a buffer between the outside world and the holy place. Worshippers did not enter the church directly from the outside but passed through the narthex before entering the church. It also served as a place where people not permitted in to the church could congregate. Fifty-two churches had an atrium standing in front of the church. Some churches had an atrium instead of a narthex, but in twenty-seven cases there were both a narthex and an atrium. This addition was probably taken over from the atrium of the Roman villa. It was an open space surrounded on all four sides by columns. It served as a place to store water used to purify those who were entering the church, or for baptismal purposes.

Since the churches were generally oriented toward the east, the entrance was in the west. In most cases there was a single entrance but sometimes there was a triple entrance, as was the case with many basilical synagogues. In many churches there were also entrances in the northern and southern walls.

The focus of ecclesiastical architecture was the interior of the building. The exterior of churches may have been pleasing to the eye, but it was their interior that was meant to dazzle the worshipper and especially the potential convert. The interior of churches was ornamented with beautiful mosaics, lamps made from precious metals, wall paintings, and intricately carved columns. The purpose of such ornamentation was to sweep the worshipper into a mystical atmosphere, an atmosphere quite unlike the outside world.

The Regional Distribution of Churches

Churches are found throughout Palestine, although they tend to be concentrated in the Judean and Samaritan hills. Galilee has the fewest churches, with Upper Galilee having only two. It is interesting to note that the opposite is true of the distribution of synagogues. The latter dominate the northern part of the country. Apparently, the Christian population center of Palestine was in the south while the Jewish population center was in the north. Another reason for the many churches in Judea was the monastic movement in Palestine. The centers of that movement were the deserts of Judea and the Negev.

Churches before Constantine

Before the reign of Constantine, ecclesiastical architecture, as such, did not exist in Palestine. This, of course, does not mean that distinctive patterns of Christian worship did not exist before that time. The Book of Acts makes it clear that the first Christians worshipped in the Temple and in the homes of community members (2:46). The Letter of James implies that Christians worshipped in places they called synagogues (Jam 2:2). Excavations at the Holy Sepulchre, the Church of the Nativity, and in other locations have shown that Christian worship sometimes took place in caves. Within three centuries, the setting of the Christian assembly changed from caves, private homes, and synagogues to stately basilicas that were built during the reign of Constantine. Excavations have clarified the Byzantine architectural tradition, but the early beginnings of the Christian assembly is still somewhat hidden from view. One problem is that Christians in Palestine did not develop their own distinctive symbol system before the fourth century. It is impossible to distinguish what may have been a place of worship used, before that date, by Jewish Christians from the Jewish synagogues. If one had only the archaeological record, the evidence would indicate that Christianity was imported into Palestine during the Byzantine period! The development of church architecture, from early forms to the introduction of the basilica, is more evident elsewhere in the Roman world than it is in Palestine. More work needs to be done, both on the literary and material remains from Palestinian Christians of the first three centuries, before we can have a clear picture of who these first Christians were, how they defined themselves, and where they worshipped.

Chapter 6

Bethlehem: The Church of the Nativity

Introduction

Some nine kilometers south of Jerusalem, just east of the road that leads to Hebron, one finds the modern city of Bethlehem. East of the Church of the Nativity there is a mound that has yielded Bronze and Iron Age pottery; therefore the identification of ancient Bethlehem with the modern city seems certain. Since there are no springs in the immediate area, the ancient town could not have supported significant settlement before cisterns were used in the hill country to collect water during the rainy season. Cisterns came into use in the late Bronze Age (1500–1100 B.C.E.).

Bethlehem is mentioned in the Hebrew Bible, the first occurence being in connection with the tomb of Rachel who is buried nearby (Gen 35:19; 48:7). The city gained prominence because of its connection with David (1 Sam 16). Despite this association, Bethlehem remained a small town—no doubt because of its proximity to Jerusalem. A highly significant text relating to Bethlehem is Micah 5:2 in which the prophet foresees greatness for the town because of its relationship to David's family: "But you, O Bethlehem Ephrathah, who are little to be among the clans of Judah, from you shall come forth for me one who is to be ruler in Israel, whose origin is from of old, from ancient days."

The Roman Period

In the Roman period (63 B.C.E.–330 C.E.) Bethlehem acquired new importance because it overlooked the roads to the fortresses at Masada and at the Herodion. When an aqueduct to Jerusalem was built, Bethlehem was able to tap into this system, lessening its complete dependence on cistern water. Of course, the New Testament presents Bethlehem as the city of Jesus' birth. The Jews were expelled from Bethlehem following the failure of the Second Revolt in 135 C.E. Apparently, Bethlehem was considered part of the territory of Jerusalem that was forbidden to the Jews by Hadrian. At this same time, the cult of Adonis, the Greek name for the Semitic god Tammuz, was encouraged by the Romans in Bethlehem. The site of this cult was above a cave venerated by Christians as the place of Jesus' birth.[1] Jerome Murphy-O'Connor believes this was an attempt to interfere with the veneration of the site by Christians, and for this reason supports the authenticity of the site. This second-century attempt to interfere with Christian worship is evidence that Christians did indeed venerate the site long before the time of Constantine.[2] Apparently, the reason for the attempt to suppress Christian worship at the place of Jesus' birth was the Romans' determination to neutralize any Jewish messianic movement. The Romans did not wish to face a third revolt inspired by a revival of messianic fervor.

The sacred site of Christ's birth, according to pious Christians, was part of a cave complex.[3] Although Matthew and Luke do not mention a cave, there are second-century Christian sources, including the apocryphal *Protoevangelium of James* (18:1), that speak about a cave in connection with Jesus' birth: "And he (Joseph) found *a cave* there and brought her (Mary) to it, and left her in the care of his sons, and went out to seek for a Hebrew midwife in the region of Bethlehem [emphasis added]."[4] Another cave located near Bethlehem in the village of Beth-Sahur was the site of a fifth-century church built to honor the memory of the shepherds who were the first to hear of Christ's birth.[5] A number of early Christian churches were built over caves including the Church of the Holy Sepulchre in Jerusalem, though this manner of worship was not considered orthodox by everyone.[6]

---

[1] Saint Jerome attests to this in his Epistle 58. He states that the cult of Adonis in Bethlehem finally was stopped by Constantine.

[2] See Murphy-O'Connor 1986, 166–67. Apparently the Romans also tried to interfere with Christian veneration of the site associated with the crucifixion and resurrection. Hadrian had a shrine to Aphrodite erected on that sacred spot.

[3] There are other caves just to the north of the one venerated as the place of Jesus' birth. Excavation has shown that they were occupied during the first two centuries of the Christian era; however, the pious association of these caves with Saint Joseph, the Holy Innocents, and Saint Jerome is without historical value.

[4] Wilhelm Schneemelcher and E. Hannecke, eds., *New Testament Apocrypha* (London: Letterworth Press, 1963) 1:383.

[5] V. Tzaferis, "The Archaeological Excavations at Shepherds' Field," *Liber Annuus* 25 (1975) 5–52.

[6] For an extensive treatment of churches built over caves see Bagatti 1971, 112–16. The fourth-century Cyril of Jerusalem implies that only the impious worship in caves while the orthodox worship in church buildings. See Migne 1863, 33:1047–48.

The Constantinian Basilica

When Constantine made Christianity the official religion of the Roman Empire, there was a rush of church building. Certainly, a church for the site of Jesus' birth was a priority. Queen Helena, Constantine's mother, dedicated the first church in Bethlehem in 339. The structure consisted of three parts (see illust. 14). There was a large (27.70 meters by 26.80 meters) atrium with a 3.5 meters wide peristyle in front of the church. The atrium opened on a square basilica (26.5 meters) with three entrances in its western wall. The internal space of the basilica was divided into five aisles by four rows of columns. At the eastern end of the basilica was the martyrium, an octagonal building (diameter of the octagon: 18.60 meters; the length of each side: 7.50 meters) that was built directly over the cave venerated as the site of Jesus' birth. There was an opening in the floor of the octagonal structure that allowed worshippers to peer into the cave.

No altar has been found here.[7] It may have been that no liturgical services were conducted in this basilica, contrary to Eusebius' claim. Its main function was to honor the place of Jesus' birth and provide an opportunity for pilgrims to catch a glimpse of the site. In the opinion of J. W. Crowfoot, there was no necessity for an altar in a church intended as a place of pilgrimage.[8] The floor of the church was covered with a colored mosaic of geometric, floral, and faunal patterns. Just one inscription survived in this Constantinian basilica: the name of Jesus is inscribed at the east end of the nave.

The plan of this church provided for a square basilica where worshippers could meet, and an octagon which housed the shrine of Jesus' birth. This architectural form is derived from the monumental mausoleums of the Roman emperors.[9] These mausoleums were not simply tombs but were tomb-temples designed to honor the dead emperor who had been raised to divinity. Constantine's architects must have thought it quite natural to adapt this form to honor Christ. The basilica attached to the octagon served merely to shelter the faithful and direct their attention to the shrine which commemorated Christ's birth. The Church of the Holy Sepulchre built under Constantine followed

---

[7] The Church of the Nativity was excavated between 1933 and 1935 by William Harvey on behalf of the Department of Antiquities of the British Mandatory Government.

[8] J. W. Crowfoot, *Early Churches in Palestine* (London: The British Academy, 1941) 27–28.

[9] Andre Grabar, *Martyrium*. (Paris: College de France, 1964) 1:245–51. Reprinted by Variorum Reprints, London, 1972; and by Krautheimer 1985, 66.

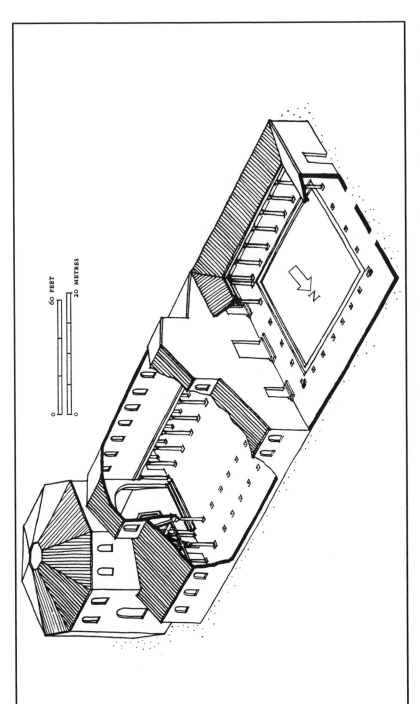

ILLUSTRATION 14. AN ISOMETRIC RECONSTRUCTION OF THE CONSTANTINIAN CHURCH OF THE NATIVITY. Note the atrium with peristyle, the four rows and columns, and the raised bema.

that same pattern, although an enclosed courtyard separated the basilica from the octagon.

Justinian's Church

Constantine's Church of the Nativity was probably destroyed in the course of the Samaritan revolt against Byzantine rule that occurred in 529, though a ninth-century source, Eutychius of Alexandria, indicated that Justinian ordered the church to be pulled down after the revolt so that he could build a much more elaborate edifice. Justinian's church certainly did surpass its predecessor in both size and beauty. The new church was enlarged in every direction (see illust. 15). A narthex was added between the atrium and church. The basilica was lengthened by a little more than seven meters so that it became rectangular rather than square. This required the erection of ten new columns. These were made to duplicate those of the Constantinian edifice and were reused in the sixth-century renovation. In place of the octagonal building of the Constantinian church, Justinian's architects added a triple apse in the form of a clover leaf at the eastern end of the basilica. The northern and southern apses formed an apsidal transept. The eastern or central apse contained a synthronos that supplied seating for the clergy. The emperor's architects also cut steps into the cave which allowed pilgrims not only to peer into the cave of Jesus' birth but also to descend into it. The interior was covered with mosaics and its ceiling was panelled.[10]

The Church of the Nativity in Succeeding Centuries

This sixth-century church building is still in use today. It managed to survive the vagaries of history in this volatile region. Many of the churches built under Justinian were destroyed during the Persian occupation of Palestine in 614. The Church of the Nativity was spared. According to a Jerusalem synod that met in the ninth century, a mosaic of the magi which adorned the church's facade was the reason the building was spared: "When the Persians, after having sacked all the towns in Syria, reached Bethlehem, they were greatly surprised to discover a representation of the Magi from Persia. Out of reverence and respect for their ancestors they decided to honor these sages by sparing the church. And this is how it has survived until this day."[11] No trace of this mosaic has survived.

[10] Crowfoot, *Early Churches in Palestine*, 84.
[11] Bargil Pixner, et al., *The Glory of Bethlehem*. (Jerusalem: The Jerusalem Publishing House, Ltd., 1981) 24.

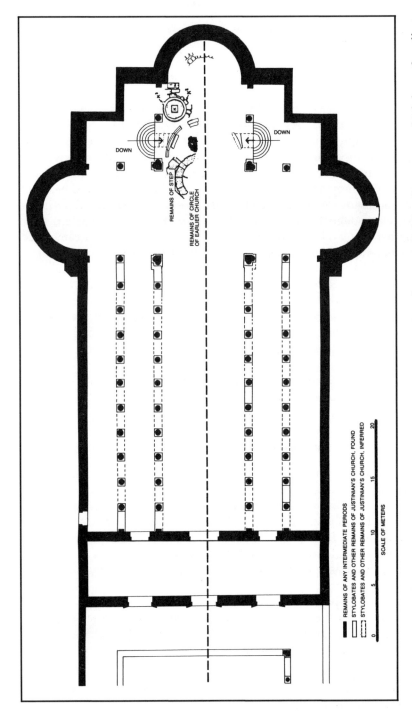

ILLUSTRATION 15. THE PLAN OF JUSTINIAN'S BASILICA OF THE NATIVITY. Note the pattern of the three apses which have the effect of a transept.

In the eleventh century, the Muslim ruler of Palestine, Hakim the Mad, was responsible for another wave of destruction which swept across Palestine. Again, the Church of the Nativity was spared because Muslims, from the time they came to Palestine, worshipped in the southern transept. They honored Jesus as a prophet and considered his birthplace an appropriate place to pray.

During the period of the Crusades, the Church of the Nativity witnessed the coronation of the crusader kings of Jerusalem. The crusaders adorned the interior of the church by painting images of their patron saints on the columns of the basilica and by decorating the walls of the nave with mosaics to replace the ones from the Justinian era. The new mosaics were crafted in the twelfth century by Byzantine artisans. Each mosaic had three registers. The mosaic along the north wall depicted, in its lowest register, the ancestors of Jesus according to Luke's genealogy (3:23-38). The middle register contained important decisions of six provincial councils. The uppermost register depicted angels. On the lowest register of the south wall were the ancestors of Jesus according to the Matthean genealogy (1:1-16). Above this, important decisions of six ecumenical councils were inscribed. Above these were mosaics of angels. The entire west wall was covered by a mosaic of the prophets with each of whom holding a text which was believed to refer to Jesus. In the transepts the mosaics depicted events from the life of Jesus. Only portions of these crusader-period mosaics have survived in to the present. The floor of the basilica, composed of stone slabs, was laid by the crusaders. One alteration the crusaders made to the exterior of the church was to partially block the central and highest portal and build a typical crusader archway leading into the narthex.

After the crusaders left Palestine, the church began to suffer. The Mamelukes who ruled from the thirteenth to the sixteenth century began looting the shrine. The looting continued under the Ottoman Turks who ruled from the sixteenth century until the beginning of the twentieth century. Carts were even wheeled into the church so that portions of its marble interior could be dismantled and taken to the Moslem shrine on the Temple mount. Some of marble that today can be seen on the Haram es-Sharif came from the Church of the Nativity. It was probably during this time that the central door of the basilica was further altered so that only a low and narrow opening remained. The two other doors of the basilica were walled up. The intent was to prevent any more looting of the church by making it difficult for thieves to leave with their booty. This alteration makes it necessary for those entering the basilica to bend their knees and head upon entering. It is impossible for an adult of normal height to walk into the church in an upright position. The building also suffered damage from an earthquake that struck in 1834, and a serious fire that ravaged the cave in 1869.

Though Justinian's church has managed to survive from the sixth century, it is hardly a shrine to the Prince of Peace. The basilica is owned by the Greek Orthodox Church. The Armenian Orthodox Church has two altars in the northern transept, and the Roman Catholics have the right to pray in the cave below the basilica at certain times but they have no rights in the basilica proper. The Franciscan Custody built the Church of Saint Catherine adjacent to the basilica to provide a larger place for worship, not only for pilgrims, but also for the local Catholic community.

The Roman Catholics celebrate Christmas on December 25, the Greeks on January 7, and the Armenians on January 19. It is a distinct blessing that these three groups do not celebrate on the same day since relations among them have not always been good. In fact, a nineteenth-century conflict between the Franciscans and the Greek Orthodox contributed to the outbreak of the Crimean War (1854–56). The Franciscans were supported by France and the Greeks by Russia. In recent years conflicts have been brewing between the Greeks and the Armenians regarding their respective control over portions of the cave.

The complex relationships between the rights of various Christian Churches to the shrines of the Holy Lands are regulated by a document called the "Status Quo." It contains the decisions the Ottoman government made toward the end of the nineteenth century, which set out the respective rights of each religious group regarding the sanctuaries each venerates. The provisions of the "Status Quo" have been enforced by all the governments controlling Palestine since then. Relationships among Christians at Bethlehem and elsewhere in the Holy Land are a cause of embarrassment. It appears as if the legacy of Christ is nothing more than real estate which is to be guarded jealously.

Despite all that has happened to the Church of the Nativity since it was first erected under Constantine and then remodeled under Justinian, the sacred edifice is a magnet that still draws the pious. It has survived wars, earthquakes, fires, pillage, and inter-Christian disputes. It is not as beautiful as it once was. Its mosaics are almost entirely gone. The simplicity of its lines is obscured by altars and baubles that the pious have set within it. Its atrium is populated by would-be guides and eager merchants. Despite all this, when a visitor enters the church itself, that person is transported into another world, a portion of which has been preserved by the survival of the Church of the Nativity.

Chapter 7

Nazareth and Capernaum: Jesus' Hometowns

Introduction

The Gospels of Matthew and Luke identify Nazareth as the town where Jesus was raised (Matt 2:23; Luke 2:51; 4:16). All four Gospels present Capernaum as an important center of Jesus' Galilean ministry. Because of their special relationship with Jesus, it is quite understandable why these two towns became important Christian centers. By the late Byzantine period impressive churches were built in each. Archaeologists have excavated, described, and even partially reconstructed these two buildings. An intriguing question about each site concerns the religious activity that went on at each site *before* the Byzantine period churches were built. Who worshipped at the sites that the Byzantines chose for their churches? Were they Jews or Christians or perhaps Jewish Christians? What kind of the structure stood on the spot of the later Byzantine churches? Were they Jewish synagogues or perhaps Christian synagogues? While the excavation and description of the Byzantine churches at both Nazareth and Capernaum have gone ahead without significant problems, interpreting the material remains of earlier occupational levels has not been without some controversy.

The churches at both Nazareth and Capernaum were excavated by Franciscans from the Studium Biblicum Franciscanum of Jerusalem. One working hypothesis that guided their interpretation of the pre-Byzantine occupation was the existence of what Bellarmino Bagatti has termed "Judeo-Christianity." Certainly there existed a type of Christianity within a Jewish context in Palestine whose adherents remained strongly influenced by Jewish beliefs and practices. This is clear enough from the literary evidence.[1] Profiling the phenomenon of Jewish Christianity can be quite complicated. For example, Raymond Brown considers the distinction between Jewish Christianity and Gentile Christianity decidedly imprecise. He suggests that the New Testament reflects at least *four* different types of Jewish/Gentile Christianity.[2] When one adds the complications that enter into this discussion with the patristic and rabbinic texts that deal with Jewish Christianity, painting a portrait of this religious phenomenon can become a difficult task. Despite these difficulties, Bagatti and his Franciscan colleagues are confident that they have uncovered archaeological evidence that can shed light on "Judeo-Christianity." This chapter first will discuss not only the Byzantine-period churches at each site but also the evidence which has led excavators at each site to suspect earlier occupation of the respective sites by "Judeo-Christians."

Nazareth

Nazareth is not mentioned in the Hebrew Bible, but the New Testament identifies it as the town where Jesus was raised and educated. Luke also states that this was the home of Mary and Joseph before the birth of Jesus (Luke 2:4-5) although Matthew implies that Bethlehem was the original home of Mary and Joseph (Matt 2). Jesus preached in the synagogue at Nazareth but was not well received. The congregation wanted to throw him off the hill on which the town was built (Matt 13:57-58; Luke 4:16-30). Although the followers of Jesus came to be known as "Christians" according to Acts 11:26, texts from the patristic period note that they were also called "Nazarenes" after the name of Nazareth.[3] There is some evidence that a Jewish-Christian community survived here into the third century.[4]

Egeria, a late fourth-century traveler, mentions no church in Nazareth but says that she saw a cave in which Mary had lived.[5] An anonymous pilgrim from Piacenza who came to Nazareth in 570 says that he visited the house of Mary which had been transformed into

---

[1] For a convenient summary of this evidence see Ernest W. Saunders, "Christian Synagogues and Jewish-Christianity in Galilee," *Explor* 3/1 (Winter, 1977) 70–73. A more detailed presentation can be found in Bagatti 1971, 3–65.

[2] See his "Not Jewish Christianity and Gentile Christianity but Types of Jewish/Gentile Christianity," *Catholic Biblical Quarterly* 45/1 (January 1985) 74–79.

[3] Migne 1863, 41:401-02. The modern Hebrew word for Christian *notzri* is likewise derived from Nazareth.

[4] Bellarmino Bagatti, O.F.M., *Excavations in Nazareth* (Jerusalem: Franciscan Printing Press, 1969) 1:14-16.

[5] John Wilkinson, *Egeria's Travels* (London: SPCK, 1971) 193.

a basilica.[6] One hundred years later, Arculf, a bishop from Gaul, wrote that he saw two churches: one where Jesus grew up and another where Mary received Gabriel.[7] The pilgrim Willibald who visited Nazareth forty years later in 724 could find only one church and it was controlled by the Moslems.[8]

The modern basilica of the Annunciation in Nazareth which was dedicated in 1968 follows the lines of a twelfth-century Crusader church. Before the construction of the modern Church was begun, Bagatti excavated beneath the Crusader remains in order to identify and describe the church of the Byzantine period (see illust. 16). Bagatti's excavations took place from 1955 to 1959. About five meters below the Crusader church, he found remains from the Byzantine period. These included a church with an atrium and a small monastery attached to the southern wall of the church. Only the foundations of the church survived. The remainder of the Byzantine church presumably was destroyed in order to make room for the much larger Crusader edifice.

Dated to the fifth century, the Byzantine church was small, eighteen by fifteen meters. It had an apse which oriented the building east to west as churches ordinarily were. A fragment of a mosaic floor in the nave is oriented to the north. The mosaic pictures a cross with the Greek letter *rho* worked into the cross suggesting the *chi-rho* abbreviation for the name of Christ. All this is within a wreath. The northern orientation of the mosaic indicates that it antedated the Byzantine church since it is highly unlikely that the mosaic's maker would have chosen this orientation when the church itself was oriented to the east. Additional evidence of an earlier use of the site came to light when excavation made it clear that the south stylobate of the Byzantine church was the wall of a preexisting structure that was simply reused by the architects in the Byzantine period. Also, a layer of fill below the church and below the adjacent monastery contained architectural fragments from a pre-Byzantine structure that resembled moldings and columns from the synagogues of Galilee and the Golan. These fragments have been dated to the middle of the third century C.E. Bagatti concluded that there was a third-century synagogue on the site of the fifth-century church. The pre-Constantinian edifice was destroyed by earthquakes some time in the late fourth or early fifth century, or perhaps it was dismantled by those who built the post-Constantinian church.

There were numerous graffiti etched on the architectural fragments of the third century building. A total of thirty-two graffiti were found.

[6] P. Geyer, *Itinera Hierosolymitana saeculi III–VIII.* (Vindobonae, 1898) 161–63.
[7] Ibid., 274.
[8] Bagatti, *Excavations in Nazareth,* 25.

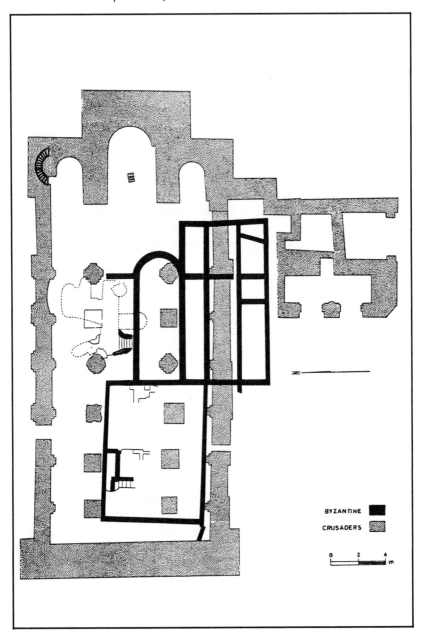

ILLUSTRATION 16. PLAN OF THE CHURCH OF THE ANNUNCIATION IN NAZARETH. The dark lines indicate the Byzantine period structures. Note the apsidal basilica in the center, the atrium in front of the church, and the monastery to the south. The lighter outline traces the Crusader church.

Most were in Greek though there were two in Syriac, two in Aramaic, and one in Armenian. Most of the graffiti are too fragmentary to read though Bagatti has identified their character as "Judeo-Christian."[9]

There is one graffito that Bagatti considers highly significant. If his deciphering of the marks inscribed on the column base is correct, the graffito may be read one of two ways, both of which are Christian. The inscribed letters are in Greek: XE MARIA (see illust. 17). The first word is an abbreviation which can be read as Christ, but Bagatti read it as an abbreviation for "hail" so that the inscription reads "Hail Mary" and is therefore a very early witness to a cult dedicated to Mary.[10] The graffito in question is not easily deciphered and certainly Bagatti's hypothesis regarding Jewish Christianity led him to read what appears to be incised Greek letters in this way. If Bagatti's reading of the graffiti etched on the plaster covering the column bases is correct, they suggest a Christian environment—not necessarily a Jewish Christian one. Bagatti concludes that a Christian presence at Nazareth before the Byzantine period had to be what he terms "Judeo-Christian."

Other finds near the *chi-rho* mosaic include some steps leading to a cave with three rooms. In one of the caves there is another mosaic floor which reads: "Gift of Conon Deacon of Jerusalem."[11] Another cave in the same area was venerated as the "Grotto of the Annunciation." It is a small room measuring 5.50 meters by 6.14 meters. No datable artifacts came to light in this room. The walls of the caves were plastered over many times and are replete with graffiti scratched in by visitors to the caves. Bagatti dates the plastered caves to the third century on the basis of similarities with the graffiti of the third-century church of Dura Europos in Syria.[12] He also notes that the cultic activities that took place in these caves resemble a similar pattern of use of caves by early Christians.[13]

Finally, below the nave of the Byzantine church, excavators discovered what appears to be a Jewish ritual bath (*mikveh*).[14] The excavators, however, have identified it as a Jewish-Christian baptistery though their is no indication that it was used by Jewish Christians. Since it was covered by the floor of the Byzantine church, it was not used after the church was built. It is also out of orientation with the earlier wall which was used to support the stylobate of the Byzantine

[9] Bagatti 1971, 126–30.

[10] Bagatti, *Excavations in Nazareth,* 156–58, and fig. 111.

[11] Bagatti, *Excavations in Nazareth,* 100.

[12] Bagatti 1971, 127.

[13] Ibid., 112–36.

[14] Bagatti, *Excavations in Nazareth,* 119–23.

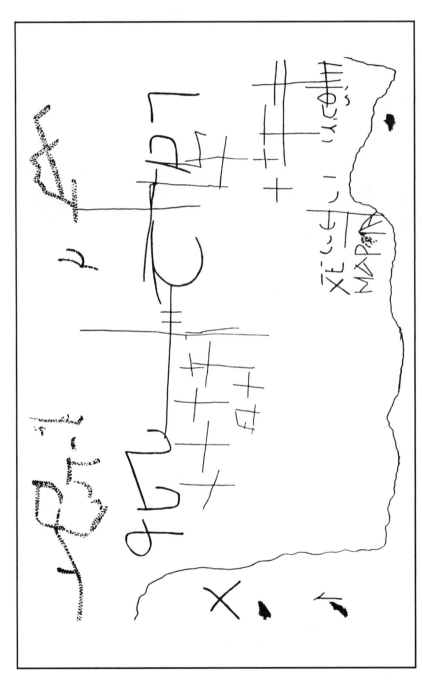

ILLUSTRATION 17. SOME GRAFFITI FOUND AT NAZARETH. The XE MARIA can be seen to the left of the crosses in the lower right corner.

church. This suggests that it was not part of the fourth-century structure. It must have been an earlier installation. Its appearance makes it likely that it was a Jewish ritual bath.[15]

These various finds led Bagatti to propose the following occupational sequence for the area once occupied by the Byzantine church: The earliest datable structure is the ritual bath that was in use until the middle of the third century. Some time later in the third century, a Judeo-Christian synagogue was built in this area. At the same time Christians began to worship in a series of caves nearby. In the fourth century, Egeria found no church but did visit the grotto of the Annunciation. In the fourth century mosaics were placed on the floor of the synagogue and in some of the caves as well. Since some of the mosaics contain crosses, it is clear that the synagogue had become a church. Around the turn of the fifth century, the remnants of the synagogue that could have been destroyed by an earthquake in 419 were dismantled, and a small church was erected in its place. The architects reused at least one wall of the synagogue. The church's nave covered the cave area and the ritual bath. This is the church seen by the pilgrim of Piacenza in 570. Attached to the southern wall of the church was a monastery below which were found many of the architectural fragments of the dismantled synagogue.

Capernaum

When Franciscan Friars Wendelin Hinterkeuser and Gaudentius Orfali began their excavations at Capernaum in 1906, they found another monumental structure in addition to the synagogue described earlier. Archaeological work was interrupted at Capernaum during World War I and it was not until 1921 that Fr. Orfali was able to continue work at the site. What was unusual about this second building was its shape: it consisted of three concentric octagons. The floor of the central octagon was decorated with a very beautiful mosaic whose centerpiece was a peacock that represents immortality in Christian iconography. Orfali identified the building as a baptistery. He took his cue not only from the mosaic but from similar buildings that can be found in Italy where baptisteries are sometimes freestanding buildings. When local guides took Christian pilgrims to Capernaum, they added a bit more color to their commentaries by naming the octagonal building "St. Peter's House."[16]

---

[15] Meyers and Strange 1981, 132, 137.

[16] Perhaps they took a clue from Egeria who reported that she saw Peter's House in Capernaum during the course of her fourth-century visit. See Wilkinson 1971, 194.

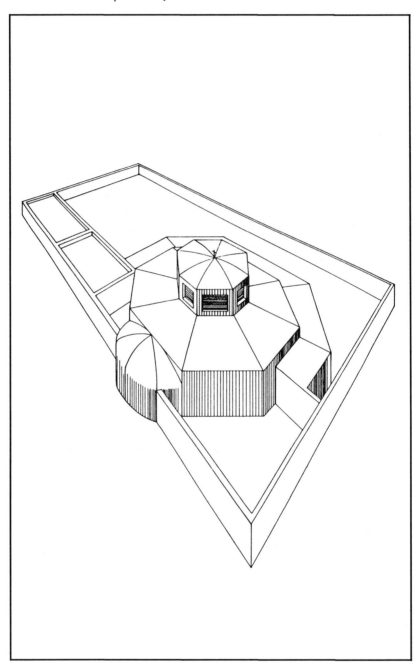

ILLUSTRATION 18. THE FIFTH-CENTURY OCTAGONAL CHURCH BUILT OVER PETER'S HOUSE.

The Gospel of Mark does speak about a house of Peter in Capernaum (Mark 1:21, 29-31). Of course, the building is clearly too ornate to have been the home of a first century fisherman. Less romantic suggestions regarding the original function of the octagonal structure consider it to have been a public fountain or the remnants of a church.

From 1968 to 1972, Fr. Virgilio Corbo of the Studium Biblicum Franciscanum of Jerusalem excavated the octagonal structure. He discovered that the outermost of the three octagons was not complete. Three of its sides were missing. Excavation of the other two octagons cleared up this mystery and confirmed the hypothesis that the structure was indeed a church. The central octagon enclosed the worship space itself. It was, in turn, enclosed by the second octagon. An apse and baptistery were attached to the second octagon. These two formed a semicircle that made it impossible to close off the third octagon (see illust. 18).

The completed structure dates to the fifth century. The date was determined by analysis of pottery and coins found in the course of excavations as well as by descriptions of the site left by early pilgrims. Antoninus Placentius speaks of a basilica on the site in 570. This would make this building the oldest centralized church in Palestine.[17] The building was probably abandoned at the beginning of the Arab period when the village was no longer occupied. A pool was built on the site during the Middle Ages.

The octagonal shape of the church indicates that it was a memorial church. The addition of the baptistery makes it clear that the church was also used by a local congregation. As a memorial church the building was designed to commemorate some event which took place at Capernaum. What memory was the church designed to preserve? Since Capernaum is mentioned frequently in the Gospels, there are a number of possibilities though the excavator is convinced that the octagonal structure was built over a first-century building that the early Christians venerated as Peter's House (see illust. 19). According to Corbo's conclusions, a private home dating from the early Roman period (63 B.C.E.–70 C.E.) was rebuilt as a shrine by Christians who used the building until the fourth century (see illust. 20). In the fifth century the octagonal building was erected over the site of the early Roman-period house. A short time later the apse and baptistery were added.

The fourth-century use of the structure is significant because of the graffiti scratched on its walls presumably by pilgrims who came to pray in the building (see illust. 21). There are well over one hundred such graffiti written primarily in Greek with a few incised in

---

[17] Asher Ovadiah and Carla Gomez de Silva 1981, 211.

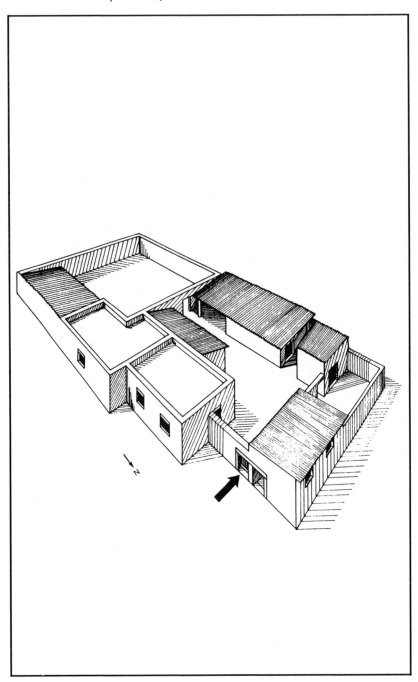

ILLUSTRATION 19. PETER'S HOUSE IN FIRST-CENTURY CAPERNAUM.

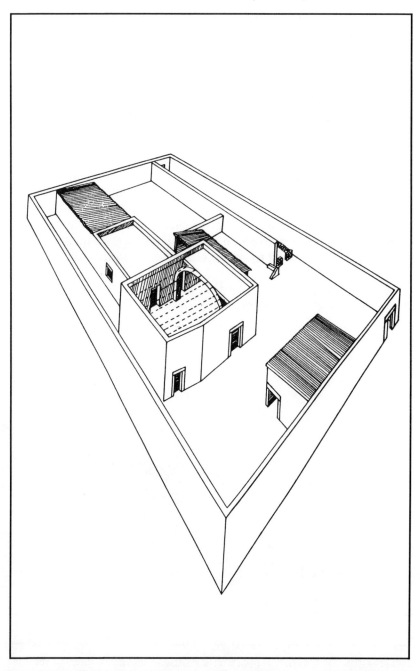

ILLUSTRATION 20. THE TRANSFORMATION OF PETER'S HOUSE TO A HOUSE CHURCH IN THE SECOND CENTURY.

Aramaic, Syriac, and Hebrew. There are two inscriptions in Latin. Some of the graffiti are obviously confessional statements about Jesus. These call Jesus "Lord" or "Messiah." This is evidence enough that the visitors to this building were Christians. Two of the graffiti have been read by Corbo as mentioning the name "Peter." They are, however, extremely difficult to decipher. This reference to Peter is just one among 131 graffiti supposedly written in five languages.[18] While an epigrapher (an expert in reading ancient inscriptions and texts) can make something out of the jumble of letters, the evidence that Peter's name is written on the walls of the fourth-century building is certainly equivocal. In any case, even if the name "Peter" were written by some pilgrim, that is not in itself the kind of evidence that would necessarily lead to the conclusion that the church was built in honor of Saint Peter. After all, the name could have been incised in the wall by a pilgrim who wished to leave behind his own name in the shrine—a practice still widely followed today by visitors to historical sites.

[18] Emmanuele Testa, *Cafarnao IV: I Graffiti della casa de San Pietro.* (Jerusalem: Franciscan Printing Press, 1972).

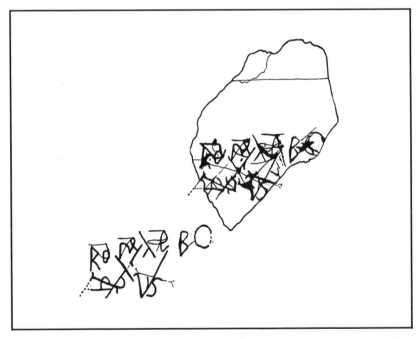

ILLUSTRATION 21. GRAFFITI FROM PETER'S HOUSE. Excavators claim to see the name Peter in Latin among this jumble of graffiti. Obviously, this reading is disputed by some.

While the presence of the name "Peter" on the graffiti in the church is difficult to establish with certainty, excavation did clarify the history of the structure on top of which the octagonal church was built. The structure was originally built at the beginning of the early Roman period (63 B.C.E.). The building was of simple construction intended for domestic purposes. It was a cluster of small rooms around a courtyard. Its walls were constructed of local basalt field stones. The only worked stones appear around the doors. The walls were not thick enough to support a second story or even a roof of masonry. The roof was probably made of mud, straw and branches (See Mark 2:1-12). The floor of the courtyard consisted of more basalt stones which were not fitted too well since there were large gaps between individual stones. The courtyard served as a work and storage area. In one corner the remains of an oven were found. This building is no different from the other houses excavated in Capernaum.

In the middle of the first century, the house underwent some significant modifications that indicate a change in usage. First, the largest room in the house had an arch built into it. This permitted the roof to be higher and to be made of masonry instead of thatch. Second, the interior floors and the walls were plastered. This was unusual for domestic buildings in Capernaum. The ceramics also indicate a change in the usage of the building. In the period before the renovations, domestic pottery types (bowls, cooking pots, jugs, pitchers, and storage jars) abound. After the plastering and other renovations, these domestic forms disappeared. Lamps and storage jars were the only ceramic remains from this second phase of the building's use. Thus, the artifacts and the architecture of the building's first phase clearly mark it as a private home. The arch, new roof, plastering, and ceramics support the conclusion that the building was no longer a private home but served some sort of public function. The graffiti suggest that this public function was a place of Christian worship.[19]

In the middle of the fifth century, the octagonal structures were built over this renovated house. Since octagonal structures were usually built to memorialize some event of Jesus' life, it is tempting to associate this house with Peter's, as mentioned in Mark 1:29. That is precisely what early pilgrims did, as is clear from the diaries they left. Fr. Stanislao Loffreda, O.F.M., Corbo's associate, suggests that identification of the building below the octagonal church as the house of Peter is "morally certain."[20] Others have concluded that a considerable body

[19] F. Graydon Synder is not ready to identify this as a pre-Constantinian house church: *Ante Pacem* (Macon, Ga.: Mercer Press, 1985) 72.

[20] S. Loffreda, *A Visit to Capernaum*, 2d ed. (Jerusalem: Franciscan Printing Press, 1973) 45.

of circumstantial evidence points to this conclusion.[21] What archaeology has demonstrated is that a private home built in the early Roman period was converted probably into a place of prayer for Christians in the middle of the first century. In the mid-fifth century a splendid octagonal church was built on the same spot. It would be fascinating to know whether the house beneath the octagonal church did in fact provide shelter to Jesus while he stayed in Capernaum, but the archaeological evidence cannot really provide an answer. Of course, the first Christian pilgrims to Capernaum scratched their confessions of faith upon the walls of this building in the belief that they were praying in the very room which Jesus called "home" at one period of his life. Nothing that has been discovered by archaeologists contradicts their belief.

In the course of excavating near the octagonal church, a small (four by five centimeters) triangular ostracon was found. It dates from the late Roman or early Byzantine period. The inscription on the ostracon is fragmentary (it consists of three lines with a total of nine characters), yet it has been adduced as archaeological support for the existence of Jewish Christianity in Palestine during this period. The only way that this inscription can be read is for the interpreter to supply letters and even entire words that make sense of the few letters that the ostracon bears. Corbo interprets the letters to be Hebrew and reconstructs the text to read: "Purify the pitcher of wine, your blood, O Yahweh."[22] On the basis of this reading, Corbo suggests that the ostracon is a fragment of a vessel used for liturgical purposes during the Christian Eucharist. That is quite a conclusion when one remembers that the text being reconstructed contains but nine letters. In his review of the Capernaum publications, James F. Strange offers another reconstruction. He suggests the text is Aramaic—a language which uses the same alphabet as Hebrew. Strange assumes that the inscription was incised on the vessel to indicate ownership, in which case the reconstructed text would have read: "N, the wine-maker; wine which he squeezed. May it be for good."[23] Strange does not maintain that his reading is definitive, but he suggests it as an alternative to Corbo's in order to show that the text can be read as an economic text rather than a cultic one.

[21] James F. Strange and Hershel Shanks, "Has the House Where Jesus Stayed in Capernaum Been Found?" *Biblical Archaeology Review* 8/6 (November/December, 1982) 37.

[22] Virgilio Corbo, O.F.M., *Cafarnao I.* (Jerusalem: Franciscan Printing Press, 1975) 107–11.

[23] James F. Strange, "The Capernaum and Herodium Publications," *Bulletin of the American Schools of Oriental Research* 226 (1977) 69.

Corbo's reconstruction of the fragmentary text is based on his assumption of the presence of a Jewish-Christian religious community at Capernaum. That there were both Christians and Jews in Capernaum is quite clear. In the Byzantine period both communities erected impressive houses of prayer. The characterization of the Christians of Capernaum as "Jewish Christians" seems quite plausible, yet it does go beyond the archaeological evidence is available. The contours of Jewish Christianity still need clarification before one can postulate the existence of such a group at Capernaum, and certainly before one can assume the existence of such a group when interpreting archaeological evidence.

Jewish Christianity

The excavations in Nazareth and Capernaum raise the issue of Jewish Christianity. The New Testament bears witness to the existence of Jewish Christian communities. The Acts of the Apostles refers to the Church in Jerusalem often. The same work describes the missions of Peter, John, and the deacon Philip in Samaritan villages (Acts 8:5-25). Summarizing the growth of the Church in Palestine, Luke wrote: "So the church throughout all Judea and Galilee and Samaria had peace and was built up; and walking in the fear of the Lord and in the comfort of the Holy Spirit it was multiplied" (Acts 9:31). Paul mentions the "churches of Christ in Judea" (Gal 1:22). The Letter of James also supports the existence of Jewish Christianity. Deploring a type of caste system that was invading the church, James wrote: "If people with gold rings and in fine clothing come into your *synagogue,* you are not to show them any deferential treatment" (Jas 2:2). In the same letter, the author uses the usual Greek word for church, *ekklesia* (5:14). That Christians used the word "synagogue" for their meeting places is significant. There are numerous other literary references to what has been described as Jewish-Christianity in both rabbinic and patristic texts.

These literary sources of knowledge about Jewish Christianity have been supplemented by material remains from Palestine. Archaeologists have been attempting to interpret the graffiti, amulets, lamps, ceramic, glass ware, decorations on tombs, and inscriptions that seem to point to the existence of Christian Jews in Palestine before the Byzantine period. At present, the archaeological remains are limited and their interpretation is debated to the extent that no consensus has emerged.

From a rabbinic point of view, Jewish Christians, could simply be considered Jews who had gone astray as long as they fulfilled the legal requirements of Jewish identity such as circumcision. The rabbis may have regarded Jewish Christians as outside the Jewish community without, however, rejecting the Jewishness of those who became Christians. According to some historians of early Judaism and Christianity, this situation changed during the Second Revolt against Rome (132–135). Because Bar Kokhba, the leader of this revolt, was seen by some as the Messiah, Jewish Christians who, of course, confessed Jesus as the Messiah refused to fight on the side of another "messiah." Bar Kokhba, therefore, attacked Jewish Christians and executed many of them. The revolt so decimated the ranks of Jewish Christians that by the end of the war Jewish Christianity had been reduced substantially. For the most part, the rabbis saw Christians as members of a different and hostile religious community rather than just Jews who had been led astray by the messianic claims made on behalf of Jesus of Nazareth.[24]

Bagatti holds that as a social-religious phenomenon Jewish Christianity lasted beyond the Bar Kokhba period. He believes that excavations at Nazareth and Capernaum demonstrate this clearly. While there is some archaeological evidence to support Bagatti's position, the argumentation at times tends to be circular. One needs to accept the hypothesis of the existence of Jewish Christianity before interpreting ambiguous evidence to support the original hypothesis. While the literary texts from both Christian and Jewish sources provide evidence for the existence of a community of Christians in Palestine who were still strongly influenced by Judaism and who were still recognized as Jews by the rabbis, the archaeological evidence that can be used to fill out the picture of this community still needs to be sifted through more carefully. The pre-Constantinian chapter of Church history in Palestine is an obscure one. The hope is that new archaeological excavations and careful study of the results will provide more insight into Jewish and Christian relationships, and the development of both Jewish and Christian identity in Palestine.

[24] Lawrence H. Schiffman, "At the Crossroads: Tannaitic Perspectives on the Jewish-Christian Schism," in *Jewish and Christian Self-Definition*, ed. E. P. Sanders (Philadelphia: Fortress, 1981) 156–57.

Chapter 8

Around the Sea of Galilee

Introduction

The region around the Sea of Galilee was the scene of much of Jesus' ministry as narrated in the Gospels. Because of this, it is not unusual to find a number of churches in the area commemorating events of Jesus' life. Beside Peter's House in Capernaum, there are at least four other memorial churches along the shore of the Sea of Galilee. Alongside the northwestern shore of the Sea of Galilee, there are memorial churches commemorating the Sermon on the Mount (Matt 5-7), the miracle of the multiplication of loaves and fishes (Matt 14:13-21; Mark 6:34-44; Luke 9:10-17; John 6:1-13), and the post-resurrection appearance before the disciples as described in John 21:1-23. Along the northeastern shore is a monastic church that has attracted pilgrims because of its association with the healing of the Gerasene demoniac (Matt 8:28-34; Mark 5:1-20; Luke 8:25-39).

There are a number of other churches in the same region which served local congregations such as the four Byzantine-period basilicas in Susita just east of the Sea of Galilee. Susita was an episcopal see with its cathedral dedicated to Saints Cosmas and Damian.[1] Along the southern shore was Beth Yerah, a town with a basilica built in the first half of the fifth century which continued to be used until the beginning of the seventh century.[2]

The missionary efforts of the early Church did not succeed in Galilee as they did in other areas of Palestine. By the Byzantine period, Galilee became the main center of Judaism in Palestine. The Jews who settled there were not about to become Christians. Despite this, Christianity must have made some gains since even in Tiberias, the prin-

[1] Ovadiah 1970, 174-78.
[2] Ibid., 40-43.

cipal Jewish center of Galilee, a church was built.[3] Western Galilee contains no sites connected with Jesus' life and ministry; consequently, the churches of that region are all of the congregational type.

This chapter will describe the memorial churches which are to be found along the shores of the Sea of Galilee. They all date to the Byzantine period when Palestine was visited by Christian pilgrims who wanted to pray at sites associated with the life of Jesus.

One issue usually raised in connection with these shrines is their historical value. The shrines that have the best claim to authenticity are those such as the Church of the Holy Sepulchre and the Church of the Nativity that were venerated by Christians already in the Roman period. Shrines whose history goes back no farther than the Byzantine period have a very doubtful claim on authenticity. The most that can be said about them is that they are places where Christians, beginning in the fourth century, began to commemorate events in Jesus' life.

The Churches of Tabgha

Not far from Capernaum is a place which was called in Greek "Heptapegon," i.e., seven springs. In Arabic this word has been corrupted to "Tabgha," the contemporary name of the site. Egeria visited this place during her travels in Palestine and though she mentioned only one church, archaeology has shown that three existed here in the fourth century (see illust. 22). Egeria's description of her visit to Tabgha reads as follows:

> Not far away from there [Capernaum] are some stone steps where the Lord stood. And in the same place by the sea is a grassy field with plenty of hay and many palms trees. By them are seven springs, each flowing strongly. And this is the field where the Lord fed the people with the five loaves and the two fishes. In fact the stone on which the Lord placed the bread has now been made into an altar. People who go there take away small pieces of the stone to bring them prosperity, and they are very effective. Past the walls of this church goes the public highway on which the Apostle Matthew had his place of custom.[4]

[3] Yoram Tsafrir, "Ancient Churches," in *Recent Archaeology in the Land of Israel*, ed. Hershel Shanks (Washington: Biblical Archaeology Society, 1981) 102. The identification of the structure in question as a church is debatable. Ancient literary sources, however, do attest that a church was built in Tiberias. Susita, Tiberias' rival city on the opposite shore, had a non-Jewish population that more readily accepted Christianity. It had four churches to serve its Christian population during the Byzantine period.

[4] Wilkinson 1971, 196, 200.

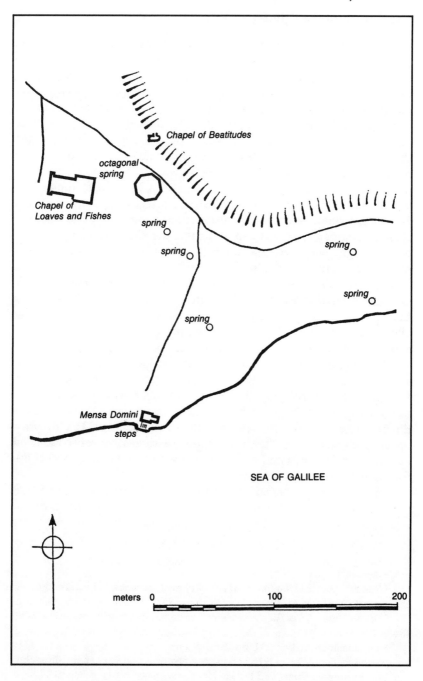

Chapel of Beatitudes

octagonal spring

Chapel of Loaves and Fishes

spring

spring

spring

spring

spring

spring

Mensa Domini

steps

SEA OF GALILEE

meters 0   100   200

ILLUSTRATION 22. THE THREE CHURCHES OF TABGHA.

The Church of the Primacy of Peter

Egeria mentions that "the stone on which the Lord placed the bread has now been made into an altar,"[5] and that people chipped away at the stone to take home relics for themselves. A. M. Schneider believed that the stone which Egeria referred to was the one under the fifth-century altar in the Church of the Multiplication of Loaves.[6] Stanislao Loffreda, the Franciscan archaeologist, identifies the rock Egeria wrote about as the worn rock with the rectangular base in the Church of the Primacy of Peter.[7] Egeria's text is somewhat ambiguous and it is hard to tell whether the stone she mentions was, in her mind, related to the resurrection appearance described in John 21 or the feeding of the five thousand (Mark 6:41). John Wilkinson suggests that originally the Tabgha site commemorated the resurrection appearance, and since the story mentions bread and fish and since the site was a small grassy plain, Tabgha was seen as a suitable place to commemorate the feeding of the five thousand. Another church in honor of this miracle was built a short distance from the Church of Peter's Primacy.[8] This site has been known as Mensa Christi (Christ's Table), Mensa Domini (the Lord's Table—see illust. 23), and the Place of the Coals (probably an allusion to John 21:9: "As soon as they came ashore they saw that there was some bread there, and a *charcoal* fire with fish cooking on it").

The chapel of Peter's Primacy, which is now in use, is a modest structure built in 1933 by the Franciscan Custody of the Holy Land. Clearly visible at the bases of the walls of this building are the walls of the early-Byzantine church that enclosed the large flat rock mentioned by Egeria. The site was partially excavated in 1933 as the present chapel was being built. More complete excavations were conducted by Stanislao Loffreda and Bellarmino Bagatti in 1968 on behalf of the Studium Biblicum Franciscanum.[9]

Before a church was built on the site, it was probably a quarry that was worked from the second to the fourth centuries. Remnants of this quarry are "the steps" which Egeria mentioned. These "steps" show the characteristic cuts made by stone masons to free limestone blocks.

[5] Ibid., 196.

[6] See his *The Church of the Multiplying of the Loaves and Fishes.* (London: A. Ouseley, 1937) 14–15, 41–42.

[7] See his *Scavi di Tabgha.* (Jerusalem: Franciscan Printing Press, 1970) 27–30, 104–5.

[8] Wilkinson 1971, 196; 200, no. 6.

[9] For a bibliography of their reports see Ovadiah and Gomez de Silva 1981, 216; and Eleanor K. Vogel and Brooks Holtzclaw, *Bibliography of Holy Land Sites,* Part II (Cincinnati: Hebrew Union College-Jewish Institute of Religion, 1982) 84.

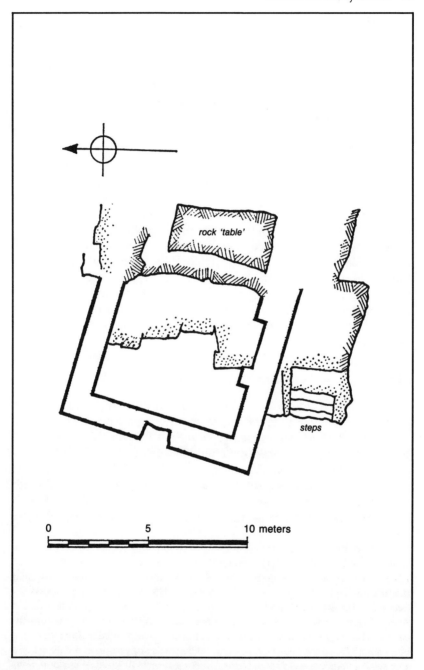

ILLUSTRATION 23. THE REMAINS OF THE FIRST MENSA DOMINI CHURCH. Note the "rock table" on which the Lord set the bread.

The excavators even found some of the implements used by the masons in their efforts to quarry the stone from this site.

At the end of the fourth century, a church contemporary with the Church of the Loaves which Egeria mentions was built on this site. Only portions of one wall and some sections of plaster remain. It is not possible to trace a plan of the building since not enough of the building has survived. In the fifth century the building was enlarged. The foundations for the southern, western, and northern walls can still be seen. There was an entrance from the west and probably entrances from the north and south as well. The walls were made of local basalt stone. The walls were especially thick which would have been unnecessary unless the ceiling was vaulted. The interior walls were covered with thick layers of plaster. The stone on which the Lord placed the bread was the focal point of the church and it probably was surrounded by an apse though no trace of an apse was found. Arculf, a seventh century pilgrim, did not see a church on this site so one can presume that it was destroyed by the Persians during their invasion in 614. The church was rebuilt at the beginning of the eighth century and was used until the thirteenth century when it was destroyed by the Baybars (1263). The Church of Peter's Primacy was used longer than the other two churches of Tabgha.

The Church of the Multiplication of Loaves

The present church built in 1980 is the most recent in a succession of churches going back to the fourth century. Egeria mentions that she saw this church in the course of her visit to Tabgha. The church that Egeria saw was built sometime after 395 (see illust. 24).[10] This building was a standard chapel comprised of one hall (17.3 by 8 meters) and an apse (2.6 meters in depth). Piers built along the north and south walls supported arches and the roof. This was typical of the Syrian style of ecclesiastical architecture. The church was not oriented directly

[10] On stylistic grounds, the church had been dated to the middle of the fourth century. See Bargil Pixner, "The Miracle Church at Tabgha on the Sea of Galilee," *Biblical Archeologist* 48/4 (December 1985) 197. Excavation, however, has determined that the edifice could not have been built before 395. A coin that was minted between 395 and 408 was found among the stone of the building's foundation. See Asher Ovadiah and Carla Gomez de Silva 1982, 130. If Egeria saw this fourth-century church this means that the date of her pilgrimage to Palestine must have been after 395. This agrees with Bellarmino Bagatti's suggestion of a date around 410; see his "Ancora sull data di Eteria," *Bibbia e Oriente* 10 73-75. Wilkinson dates Egeria's travels in Palestine between 381 and 384; see his *Egeria's Travels* (1971) 2, 9, 237-39.

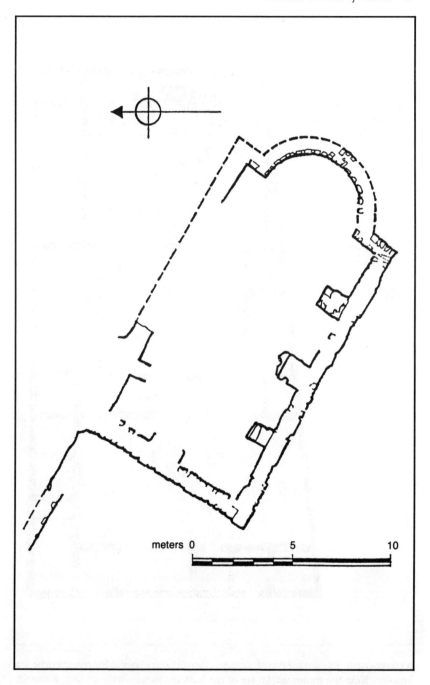

ILLUSTRATION 24. THE FIRST CHURCH OF THE MULTIPLICATION OF LOAVES.

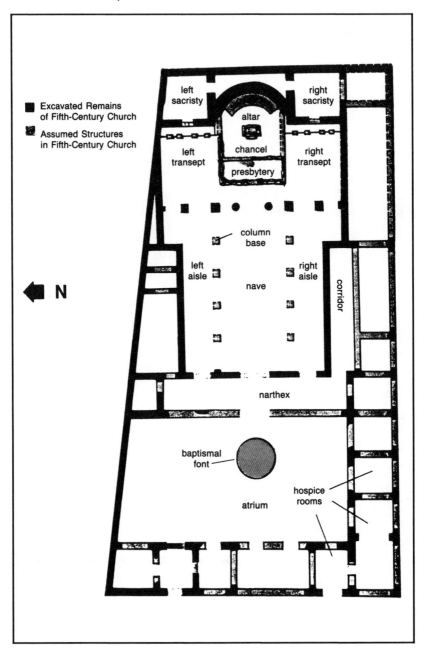

ILLUSTRATION 25. THE FIFTH-CENTURY BASILICA OF THE MULTIPLICATION OF LOAVES. Note the trapezoidal form of the building in which the church is found. Note also the narthex and atrium in front of the church.

toward the east but was inclined some twenty-eight degrees to the south.

This fourth-century church could have been erected by Joseph of Tiberias, the Jewish Christian honored by Constantine with the title of count and who was commissioned by him to erect a number of churches in Galilee for the Jewish Christian community. According to the account of Bishop Epiphanios of Salamis, Joseph built churches in Sepphoris, Nazareth, Tiberias, and Capernaum.[11] Since the church at Capernaum had not yet been built, it is likely that Joseph used his license to build at Capernaum for this project in Tabgha which is just a short distance away.

During the second half of the fifth-century the church was extensively remodeled (see illust. 25). The worship space was enlarged (29.6 by 15 meters) and the apse was set so that worship was oriented toward the east. This required that the stone "on which Jesus sat" be moved and installed under a new altar in the center of the sanctuary which was raised one step above the rest of the church. The area dedicated to worship was located within a larger trapezoidal structure. The building's somewhat odd shape was dictated by its proximity to a major thoroughfare that ran just north of the building. This required that the building's northern wall be built at an angle to avoid running into the road that was just outside the church.[12] The larger structure housed the church, an atrium, and hospice rooms for pilgrims. On the north side of the apse was the prothesis and on the southside was the diaconicon. These two rooms were connected by a corridor running behind the apse, a feature which is unusual in the churches of Palestine. A semicircular synthronos abutted the inner wall of the apse. The building also had an internal rectangular transept that also was an unusual feature in churches of this period in Palestine although there are parallels in Algeria, Egypt, and Nubia.[13] The building was constructed of local, crudely cut basalt stone.

Though the building's external architecture was not very impressive, a masterpiece was created for its interior space. The nave of the church was covered with a colored mosaic with geometric patterns and motifs of plant and animal life (see illust. 26). In the transept the mosaic depicts scenes of flora and fauna that are native to the region surrounding the Nile River together with architectural diagrams and a

---

[11] Migne 1863, par. 410–11.

[12] The building's north wall was built on an angle to avoid a road that ran nearby as well as the aqueduct beside it (Ovadiah 1970, 57). The road was probably a branch of the Via Maris that connected Egypt and Syria located in the region.

[13] Pixner, "The Miracle Church," 200.

ILLUSTRATION 26. ONE OF THE MOSAICS IN THE FIFTH-CENTURY BASILICA OF THE MULTIPLICATION OF LOAVES. The bell-like lotus flower is not found in Palestine but is native to Egypt.

nilometer (a device used to determine the depth of the Nile River). Finally, behind and to the east of the altar was a mosaic of a basket with four loaves of bread in a basket. On either side of the basket was a fish.[14]

There were also two Greek inscriptions set into the mosaic floor. One of these names the artist (a certain Saurus who is otherwise unknown) and the other names Patriarch Martyrios, a patron of the church. Though the latter inscription is incomplete it has been read as follows: "To the memory and the repose of the sponsor, the holy Patriarch Martyrios."[15] If this reading is correct, the reason for the Egyptian motifs in the mosaic become clear. Martyrios, who was patriarch in Jerusalem from 478 to 486, lived in Egypt as a young man. When he decided to beautify the Church of the Multiplication of Loaves, he hired an Egyptian artist. This inscription also helps date the renovation of the church since it was obviously completed after Martyrios' death.

The church was destroyed in the seventh-century during the course of the Persian and Arabian incursions into Palestine when Byzantine control over the region came to an end. Arculf, the French bishop and pilgrim who visited Tabgha around 670, found no building but only a few columns remaining.[16] The site was forgotten until the end of the nineteenth century when a portion of the mosaic was discovered by accident. Excavations began in 1911 by Paul Karge whose work was interrupted by the Turkish government. Unfortunately, a final report on Karge's excavations was never published. In 1932 Andreas E. Mader and Alfons Maria Schneider began a series of excavations which not only revealed the mosaics of the sixth-century basilica but also revealed the existence of the first church built at the beginning of the fifth century.[17] The early church building was reexamined in 1970 by Stanislao Loffreda.[18] In 1933 a temporary structure was erected over the mosaics to help preserve them and to serve the needs of pilgrims and visitors to the site, and in 1980 a new church was dedicated at Tabgha. The modern church was built according to the architectural style of its Byzantine period predecessor.

[14] For a more detailed description of the mosaics with color illustrations see Dodo Joseph Shenhav, "Loaves and Fishes Mosaic Near Sea of Galilee Restored," *Biblical Archaeology Review* 10/3 (May/June 1984) 22–31.

[15] Pixner, "The Miracle Church," 201.

[16] D. Baldi, *Enchiridion Locorum Sanctorum.* (Jerusalem: Typis PP. Franciscanorum, 1935), p. 276.

[17] For a bibliography of reports on these excavations, see Ovadiah 1970, 59.

[18] S. Loffreda, "Sondaggio nella chiesa della moltiplicazione dei pani a Tabgha" *Liber annuus* 20 (1970) 370–80.

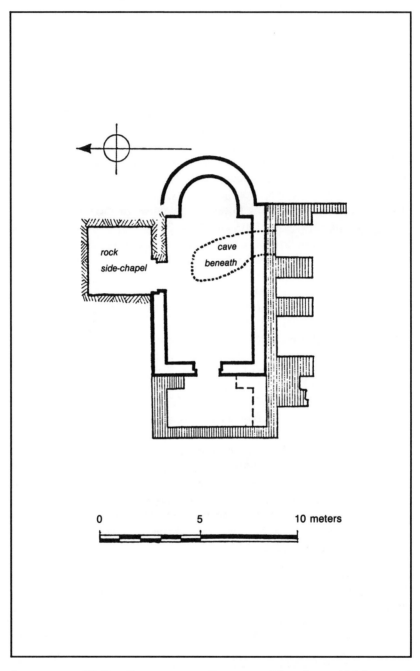

ILLUSTRATION 27. THE CHURCH OF THE BEATITUDES Note the apsidal form and the cave below the church.

The Church of the Beatitudes

Just three hundred meters north and east of the Church of the Multiplication of Loaves are the ruins of another fourth century church: the Church of the Beatitudes (see illust. 27). Beneath the church is a cave which recalls Egeria's description: "Near there on a mountain is the cave to which the Savior climbed and spoke the Beatitudes."[19] The site was excavated in 1935 by Bellarmino Bagatti on behalf of the Studium Biblicum Franciscanum.[20] He came upon the church in the course of his excavations of the cave mentioned by Egeria. This church was part of a monastic settlement and therefore was rather small (9.25 by 4.40 meters). It had an apse at the east end and an atrium in front of its western entrance. The floor was covered with a mosaic of floral and geometric patterns. Scratched on the walls of the chapel were some crosses. Only fragments of its altar were found. Bagatti dates the church to the sixth century. The settlement was destroyed in the seventh century by the Persians and the church was never rebuilt. In 1938 a new church was built to commemorate the Sermon on the Mount but not on the site of the sixth century church. The modern church at the top of the hill commands a beautiful view of the Sea of Galilee. The view encompasses all the sites around the Sea of Galilee where Jesus preached and lived.

Kursi

Beginning in the fifth century a large Byzantine monastic complex on the eastern shore of the Sea of Galilee became a place of pilgrimage. It is assumed that the pilgrims came here to visit the place where Jesus cast out demons from a possessed person and sent them into some swine who ran headlong into the Sea of Galilee (Matt 8:23-34; Mark 5:1-21; Luke 8:32-37). Ancient manuscripts of the Gospels give three different names for the site of this exorcism: Jerash, Gadara, and Gergesa. The first two are in Transjordan and are quite a distance from the Sea of Galilee. Gergesa has never been identified. Saint Jerome confused this name with that of the village of Korazim which is on the other side of the lake. It is assumed that Kursi is a corruption of Korazim. This site was excavated between 1970 and 1972 by V. Tsaferis and Dan Urman on behalf of the Israel Department of Antiquities.[21]

---

[19] Wilkinson 1971, 200.

[20] For a bibliography on the site see Ovadiah 1970, 60.

[21] For a bibliography on the site, see Ovadiah and Gomez de Silva 1981, 240, and Vogel and Holtzclaw 1982, 52.

Recently, the site has been restored and made part of the Israeli National Park system.

The church is part of a larger monastic complex that is surrounded by a great rectangular wall (145 by 123 meters). In antiquity the wall was plastered. There was only one gate in this wall. The gate was strongly fortified and faced the lake. The gate opened to a street that led directly to the church which was in the center of the settlement. In front of the church was an atrium. The atrium was surrounded by a peristyle the eastern part of which served as a narthex. In the center of the atrium was a cistern. The church was an apsidal basilical with two rows of six columns each that divided the interior space into a nave and two aisles. On either side of the apse is the pastophoria. The columns supported very beautiful Corinthian capitals. In the apse is the synthronos that is on that sanctuary platform which is two steps above the nave. The diaconicon was later converted into a baptistery. On either side of the two aisles are chapels and auxiliary rooms.

The floor of the apse was covered with marble. The floor of the nave, aisles, chapels, and auxiliary rooms were covered with mosaics which have floral, faunal, and geometric patterns. When the Moslems reused the church for private dwellings after the eighth century they systematically defaced the animal and bird patterns on the mosaic because their religious sensibilities were offended by images of living things. Under the floor of the chapel on the south side, there was a small crypt where the monks were buried. Since there was room for just three bodies, presumably the bodies would be placed in the crypt until desiccated. The bones were removed and buried elsewhere when room in the crypt was needed for another body.

An inscription in the baptistery dates the reuse of the diaconicon to 585 during the reign of Emperor Maurice, and names the head of the monastery as a certain Stephanus. Ceramics indicate that the building was in use from the middle of the fifth century. It was damaged but not abandoned during the Persian invasion. The building was renovated and remained in use until the eighth century when it was destroyed by fire. Local Arabs used the ruins of the structure for their own purposes and were responsible for mutilating the mosaic.

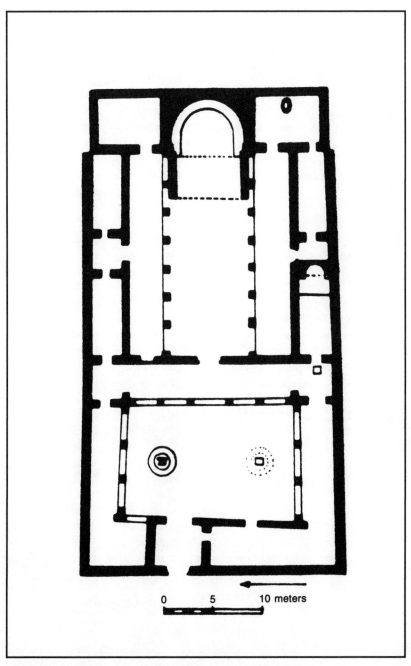

ILLUSTRATION 28. THE CHURCH AT KURSI. Note the single apse and the atrium with peristyle.

ILLUSTRATION 29. SITES OF CHURCHES FROM THE BYZANTINE PERIOD. Note how they cluster in the Jerusalem area and in the south.

Chapter 9

The Churches of Jerusalem

The Emperor Hadrian banned Jews from Jerusalem following the Bar Kochba revolution (132–135). After the failure of this Second Revolt against Rome, Jerusalem was no longer a Jewish city. Jews could not reside in Jerusalem until the Empress Eudocia pressured the imperial government to permit their resettlement in the city some four hundred years later. Hadrian renamed Jerusalem "Aelia Capitolina" to honor both the Capitoline Jupiter and his own family, the *Aelii*. Hadrian wanted to transform Jerusalem even before the outbreak of the Jewish insurrection. Rumors of his plans sparked Bar Kochba's revolt. With the defeat of the Jews there was no obstacle standing in the way of Hadrian's plans. He built a temple to Venus on the site of what would be the Church of the Holy Sepulchre. Jerusalem became a center of Roman religion. It remained so for almost two hundred years.

With the triumph of Constantine in 313, Jerusalem changed character again. Jerusalem became a Christian city. The Christians from Byzantium built churches and monasteries in the city and its environs. Hospices went up to care for the spate of pilgrims that began to converge on the city. The object of their journey was to see the place of Jesus' crucifixion and resurrection. What they saw when they came to Jerusalem was impressive: Constantine had built three beautiful structures right off the city's main thoroughfare. These buildings enshrined Calvary and the tomb of Jesus.

Despite its importance as a center for pilgrims, Jerusalem had no political status. The capital of Roman Palestine was Caesarea and it remained so under the Byzantines. Caesarea was also the most important ecclesiastical center in the region. It was not until 451 that Jerusalem became the seat of a metropolitan patriarch who oversaw seventy other bishops. The glory of Jerusalem during the Byzantine period was not its political or ecclesiastical status. Its churches, built and beautified by members of the imperial family, were what astounded the pilgrims who came to the Holy City (see illust. 29).

Fourth Century Buildings

The Church of the Holy Sepulchre

Because Jerusalem was the scene of Jesus' death and resurrection, it had a powerful attraction for pilgrims. Several churches were built there to accommodate local congregations and to serve the needs of pilgrims. The most important of these churches was the Church of the Resurrection now known as the Church of the Holy Sepulchre. The present structure is essentially a Crusader building. The earlier Byzantine church was destroyed under the Caliph Hakim in 1009. It was this act that give first impetus to the Crusades. After Hakim's death, the new caliph authorized the rebuilding of the church. Monomachus, the patriarch of Jerusalem, rebuilt the shrine over the tomb of Jesus and built a small chapel on Calvary in 1048. This was not enough to placate European Christians. They took control of Jerusalem from the Arabs in 1099 and began building a new church to enclose Calvary and the tomb of Jesus. It was the Crusaders who gave the church its present name. The Byzantines called their church *Anastasis* (resurrection).

Excavation of this site is difficult because the church is currently in use. Every day thousands of pilgrims pass through it. In addition, the tensions between the various Christian denominations that control individual parts of the structure make a systematic excavation project almost a practical impossibility. Still, William Harvey made some trial soundings in 1933–34 on behalf of the British Mandatory Government.[1] In 1961 and 1963 Virgilio Corbo, O.F.M. reexamined the structure.[2] These excavations made it clear that this site was outside the city until Hadrian built the Roman Aelia Capitolina about one hundred years *after* the death of Jesus. Excavations also show that the area occupied by the church was a former stone quarry used for tombs when the quarry was no longer in use. The hill of Calvary was an isolated acclivity resulting from the work of the ancient stone cutters. They worked around a serious flaw in the stone and the result was a formation that looked like a human skull.

The site of the church built in the early-Byzantine period was that of Hadrian's temple to Venus. Even though the Gospels state that Jesus was crucified outside the walls of Jerusalem, the location chosen for the church of the Holy Sepulchre was far inside the fourth-century walls. From the perspective of the Byzantine Christians the site cho-

[1] W. Harvey, *Church of the Holy Sepulchre, Jerusalem* (Oxford: Oxford University Press, 1935).
[2] V. Corbo, "Plans and Section," *Liber Annuus* 12 (1961–62) 221–316, and 14 (1963–64) 293–338.

sen for the church did not jibe with the details given in the Gospels, but the pull of local tradition about the location of Jesus' tomb was too strong. The Byzantine Christians may not have realized that the site they chose for their church was outside the city walls in Jesus' day. That the tradition regarding the site of Jesus' death and burial antedates the Byzantines supports its authenticity. Apparently, Christians honored the site from the beginning of the Church's existence. Some maintain that Hadrian built a temple to Venus on the site in 135 precisely to discourage Christian veneration. According to Eusebius, the fourth-century bishop of Caesarea and the first church historian, the temple was torn down in 326; and Makairos, the bishop of Jerusalem, identified one of the tombs in the area as that of Jesus. Constantine ordered the building of a great church to honor the site. It was dedicated on September 17, 335. The pre-Constantinian tradition about the site of Jesus' tomb testifies to the existence and strength of the Jewish Christian community in Jerusalem. With the arrival of the Byzantine Christians and their bishops, the indigenous Christian community was absorbed by the new Christian community. The pre-Constantinian Christian community of Jerusalem left a precious legacy: their memory of the location of Jesus' tomb.

The original church built by Constantine consisted of two buildings connected by a great porticoes courtyard (see illust. 30). One building was a basilica. This was the setting for liturgical assembly. The second building was an elaborate structure carved out of the limestone that enclosed the tomb of Jesus. Though very little of either structure remains, we have some idea of what they looked like, since Eusebius provided a detailed description of both buildings.

Understandably, the basilica was more elaborate than most. A triple doorway led from the Cardo Maximus, Jerusalem's main thoroughfare, to an atrium. After passing through the atrium, the worshipper entered the basilica proper through one of three doors. Five naves created by four rows of columns made up its interior space. The height of the central nave was about twenty-two meters. At 13.5 meters in width, it was the widest of the five aisles. There was a single apse ornamented with twelve columns that were capped by large silver urns. There are some remains of a colored mosaic floor with geometric patterns. Colored marble covered the facade. The limestone of the other exterior walls was highly polished to make it look like marble. The interior walls were faced with multicolored marble. Unlike the other churches in Palestine, the Church of the Resurrection was oriented to the west rather than to the east. The topography of the area and the location of the tomb probably dictated this.

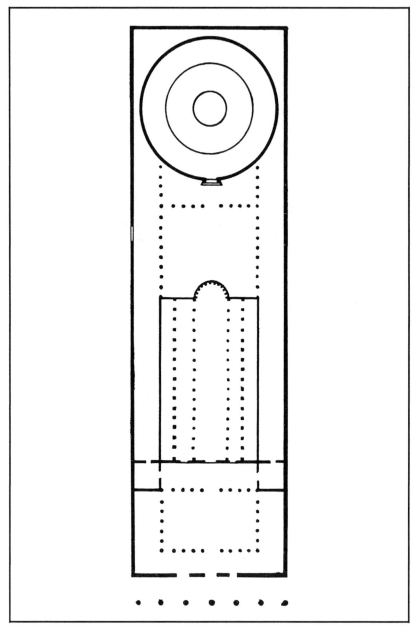

ILLUSTRATION 30. THE CHURCH OF THE RESURRECTION (THE HOLY SEPULCHRE) BUILT BY CONSTANTINE. The structures enclose the place of the crucifixion (Golgatha) and the tomb of Jesus. This drawing is based on the description of Eusebius.

The tomb of Jesus was enclosed in a circular building forty-eight meters in circumference. Its wooden roof was sealed with lead. Worshippers were able to walk around the western part of the building because of a semicircular ambulatory with a diameter of thirty-five meters. The dome of the building over the tomb was supported by twelve columns and eight piers. The latter were arranged in pairs at the cardinal points. The tomb itself was beneath the dome. The tomb was not aligned with the church but with Calvary.

There are similarities between this building and Roman mausoleums such as the Constantia Mausoleum in Rome. It is clear from the attached church that the Byzantines did not see this structure as a memorial to someone who died but a monument to the triumph of the resurrection.

The Persians who invaded Palestine in 614 destroyed the Constantinian basilica. In 626, Modestus, the patriarch of Jerusalem, built another church over the site of Calvary and the tomb of Jesus. His church was larger and configured differently from the Constantinian one. The principal difference was that Modestus had an enclosed atrium connecting the church and the tomb. He built a circular structure above the tomb. On the perimeter of this structure there were semicircular recesses on the north, south, east, and west sides (see illust. 31). A second difference was that the church and the tomb were both enclosed within a larger building. Modestus' church, like its predecessor, was oriented toward the west. Because little remains of this church, its description is dependent upon the diary of Arculf, the Gallic bishop who came to Jerusalem as a pilgrim.

When the Muslims wrested control of Palestine from the Byzantines in the seventh century, a treaty guaranteed the sanctity of all Christian holy places in Jerusalem. The Church of the Resurrection and the tomb of Christ remained untouched for three hundred years. The tenth century witnessed some vandalism but nothing like the wholesale destruction decreed by the Caliph Hakim. On October 18, 1009, an act of anti-Christian fanaticism ordered by Hakim resulted in the complete destruction of the church and the obliteration of the tomb of Jesus. Portions of the rotunda over the tomb survived and can be seen today.

In the eleventh century, the rotunda above the tomb was restored, but the church remained in ruins. When the Crusaders captured Jerusalem, they set about rebuilding the church. It was dedicated on July 15, 1149. The Crusaders kept the building over the tomb of Jesus intact while restoring the church to its original Constantinian dimensions. It is this church that the visitor to Jerusalem sees today.

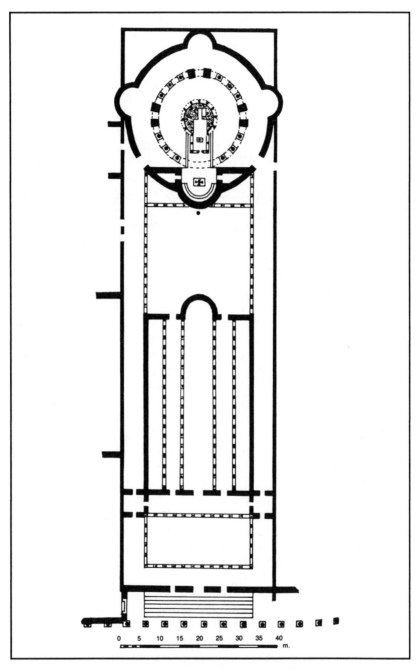

ILLUSTRATION 31. THE CHURCH OF THE RESURRECTION (THE HOLY SEPULCHRE). This drawing is based on the account of Arculf the pilgrim.

The Eleona Church

Another site in Jerusalem that attracted Constantine's attention was the Mount of Olives. While there were several churches built there, the principal one was known as the "Eleona" Church (see illust. 32). (Eleon was the Greek name of the Mount of Olives. Its pronunciation in the local dialect was Eleona.) This church was large (30.5 by 19 meters). It was on a platform. Worshippers had to climb several steps to reach a small (19 by 3.5 meters) portico with six columns at its facade. The portio opened to an atrium (25 by 19 meters) that was encircled by a peristyle. In its center was a cistern. The church was a basilica whose interior space was divided into a nave and two side aisles by two rows of columns (six to a row). The altar was on a platform that was reached by two stairways. Behind the altar was an exterior polygonal apse. Below the platform was a crypt that was reached by way of a staircase from within the church. The crypt was cut from the limestone bedrock. The pious believed that Jesus taught his disciples in the crypt. The floor of the church was covered by a colored mosaic. It was decorated with floral and geometric patterns.

Descriptions of this Constantinian church come from Eusebius and the Bordeaux Pilgrim (fourth century).[3] It was destroyed by the Persians in 614 and rebuilt later. It was excavated in 1910 by L. H. Vincent on behalf of the *École biblique*.[4] Today, it is the site of the Pater Noster church. It is so named because of the pious belief that Jesus taught his disciples the Lord's Prayer in the crypt. In the cloisters of this church there are plaques with the Lord's Prayer written in many languages.

Constantine called this building "the Church of the Disciples and the Ascension." It was one of three churches he built over caves. The other two are the Church of the Nativity and the Anastatis (Holy Sepulchre). By 384 another church memorializing the ascension of Jesus was built farther up the hill.

The Church of the Ascension

According to Luke, Jesus ascended into heaven from somewhere in Jerusalem (Luke 24:50-52). The Byzantines located the site of the ascension on the Mount of Olives and built a church to memorialize

[3] *Revue biblique* 64 (1957) 48-71.

[4] The Bordeaux Pilgrim was an anonymous French traveller to the Holy Land who apprently made his journey just before the beginning of the Byzantine period (early fourth century A.D.). He produced the first book describing a tour through the Holy Land. He may not have visited all the places he lists since most of his information appears to be copied from Jewish sources.

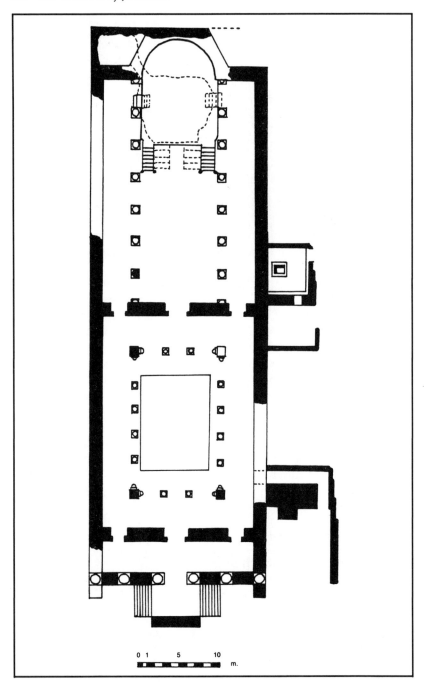

ILLUSTRATION 32. THE ELEONA CHURCH ON THE MOUNT OF OLIVES.

the event (see illust. 33). The project was financed by Poimenia, a pious Roman woman. The church did not serve a local congregation so it could be built in the form of an octagon. There was a portico along the western wall of the church. There were entrances from both the east and west. The altar probably stood opposite the eastern entrance. There were sixteen columns that surrounded the building and supported its domed roof. The diameter of the building was thirty-five meters. In the center of the church was a rock that supposedly bore the footprints of Jesus left before he ascended into heaven. The current structure on the site is a mosque, and the Muslim curators show visitors the "footprints" of Jesus.

The Church of the Ascension stood until the Persian invasion in 614. Modestus, the patriarch of Jerusalem, built another church on the spot in the first half of the seventh century. Arculf, who wrote of his visit to Jerusalem in 670, described the Church of the Ascension. Only a few remnants of the church were found. Apparently, the building was circular. Its interior diameter was 26.5 meters. Excavators found part of a Greek inscription that identifies the site as the place of the Ascension, and Modestus as the builder of the church standing on the site.

Gethsemane

Another church on the Mount of Olives is a memorial to the agony and arrest of Jesus (see illust. 34). Excavations by Pietro Orfali, O.F.M., took place in 1919–20 in preparation for the building of the Church of All Nations that currently occupies the site identified by Christians as the Garden of Gethsemane. During these excavations the remnants of the Byzantine church was found beneath the ruins of the Crusader edifice. The twentieth-century church replaces the one built by the Crusaders in the twelfth century. Before Orfali's excavations it was believed that the Crusader church stood exactly above the ruins of the fourth-century church. The Byzantine church was two meters lower than the Crusader church and its axis was about thirteen degrees north of the current church which follows the lines of the twelfth-century building. Visitors to the Church of All Nations can see this for themselves since there are gaps in the modern floor revealing the Byzantine floor below. The floor of the fourth-century church was decorated with colored mosaics bearing floral and geometric patterns.

The church was probably built by the Emperor Theodosius I and was dedicated in 385. It incorporated a large rock that the pious identify as the rock on which Jesus prayed. An earthquake destroyed this church in 747. The crusaders built a church here in 1170. It appears

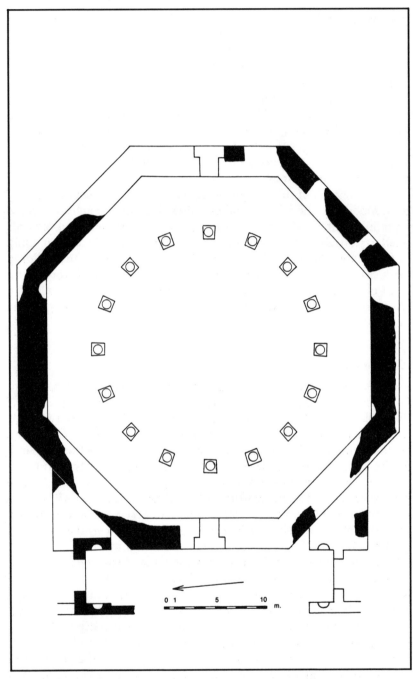

ILLUSTRATION 33. THE CHURCH OF THE ASCENSION ON THE MOUNT OF OLIVES.

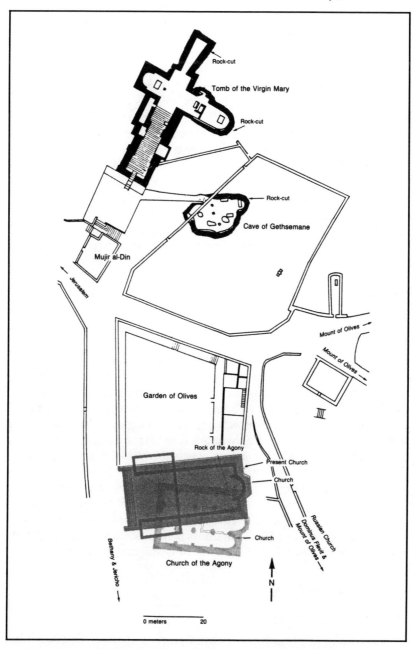

ILLUSTRATION 34. CHURCHES AT GETHSEMANE. The church at the top is built over the tomb of Mary. The church at the bottom is built around the rock in the Garden of Olives on which Jesus prayed.

to have been abandoned in the fourteenth century. The church that pilgrims visit today was built in 1924.

The Church of Holy Zion

On the Madaba map this church appears to be larger than the Church of the Holy Sepulchre. Literary sources call this church "the mother of all the churches of Zion." The church was located on Mount Zion near the present Dormition Abbey and Tomb of David. Only a few remnants of the church were uncovered in the course of partial excavations by H. Renard in 1899. There are many descriptions of this church in literary sources. The excavator estimated the length of the church to be fifty-five meters. Literary sources mention a portico attached to a basilica that had a central nave and two side aisles on either side. These were created by four rows of columns supported on stylobates. There was a triple apse. There were at least two stages in the construction. The first was at the end of the fourth century. After the Persian invasion, Modestus rebuilt the church in 634. The seventh-century church remained standing when in 966 Arabs looted and burned it.

The Tomb of Lazarus

The Arab town of el 'Eizariya (the New Testament Bethany) derives its name from Lazarus whom Jesus raised from the dead (John 11). It is located three kilometers east of Jerusalem along the Jerusalem-Jericho road. The Byzantines built a basilica over the tomb venerated as Lazarus' tomb. While an exact date cannot be given, the church was standing by 390 since Jerome mentions it in his translation of Eusebius' *Onomasticon* published in that year. It was an apsidal basilica that measured thirty-four by seventeen meters. It was decorated by a mosaic with geometric patterns. This church was destroyed by an earthquake and replaced by a larger one in the fifth century. Both churches abutted the tomb of Lazarus. The church that visitors see today was built by the Franciscans in 1952. Trap doors just inside the doorway of the modern church reveal portions of both Byzantine churches.

Fifth Century Buildings

The Church of Saint Stephen

According to pious belief of the Byzantine period, Stephen was martyred outside the Damascus Gate. Just a short distance from that gate, the Empress Eudocia built a church in honor of Saint Stephen in the fifth century. The church was excavated in the nineteenth century before the present basilica of Saint Etienne was built. This church serves the Dominican community of the *École biblique*. The church was a basilica that measured thirty-eight by nineteen meters. It had an atrium and a polygonal apse. Its interior space was divided into a central nave and two side aisles by two rows of columns. Apparently, there were six columns in each row. A few Corinthian and basket capitals have survived. The ancient church served a monastery that stood next to it.

The Church of John the Baptist

Apparently, the Empress Eudocia also built a church in honor of John the Baptist in Jerusalem. Though this church cannot be credited to her with certainty, its masonry and construction were similar to churches that we know the empress built. This was a small church with an unusual plan that served monks who lived nearby. It had a narthex (21.5 by four meters) which one entered through any one of three entrances in the west wall. The church itself was trefoil in shape: there was one central apse and two side apses. These three apses produced an internal apsidal transept. It measured twenty-one by twelve meters. Along the western and eastern walls and at the extremes of the apse chords, there were four piers that supported the building's dome. The sanctuary was one step above the floor level of the nave. It was surrounded by the central apse in the center of which stood the altar. Below the church was a crypt hewn out of the limestone upon which the church was founded. This church is located a short distance from the Church of the Holy Sepulchre.

The Tomb of Mary

The Kidron Valley was a favorite place for burials. Its location at the foot of the Mount of Olives made it an ideal place for tombs. The Jews believed that the resurrection of the dead would begin when the Messiah descended from the Mount of Olives, crossed the Kidron Valley, and entered the Temple. Christians, too, began to bury their dead in the Kidron. In the fifth century the Byzantines built a church over the site where the pious located the tomb of Mary, the mother of Jesus. The church was octagonal and Mary's tomb was on the east side of the octagon. The diameter of the building was 15.1 meters. The interior of the church was adorned with a circular colonnade that was nine meters in diameter.

Sixth Century Buildings

Saint George

Near the Givat Ram campus of the Hebrew University, Michael Avi-Yonah uncovered a church that once served a monastery. It was a small building (15 x 12.7 meters). It was decorated with a mosaic floor that contained a dedication to Saint George near the apse. It was built at the beginning of the sixth century by Empress Eudocia.

The Nea Church

The word "Nea" is Greek for new. Justinian built a "new church" in 543 in honor of Mary the Mother of God. It faced the cardo of the Byzantine city. It was the largest church in Palestine. It was 116 meters long and 52 meters wide. It was a basilica with a central nave and two side aisles (see illust. 35). It was oriented to the east by a triple apse. Its interior walls were covered with marble. Little of this building remains except a portion of the eastern apse discovered by Nahum Avigad while excavating in the Jewish Quarter. Literary sources assert that the church was part of a larger complex that included a monastery, library, hostel, and hospital. None of these structures have been found or identified. The eastern apse of the church has been preserved under the Jewish Quarter and can be visited today.

Conclusions

Eusebius states that until the time of Hadrian there was a very large church in Jerusalem built by Jewish Christians. By Eusebius' day (fourth century) the location of this church was a fading memory. Eusebius complained that he could find no records of it. Indeed, the Jewish Christian community of the first centuries in Palestine is still a mystery not clarified by archaeological excavations. With the triumph of Constantine, the church in Palestine changed. Its membership and leadership was Gentile. These Gentile Christians left an indelible reminder of their presence in Jerusalem by building many churches. Several of these churches were destroyed during the Persian sack of Jerusalem in 614. The Byzantine Christians rebuilt these churches, which continued to serve the needs of the local Palestinian church and pilgrims during the Muslim period. In the eleventh century many churches in the Jerusalem area were destroyed or severely damaged because of the policies of the Caliph Hakim. It was these actions that set off the Crusades. Although Hakim's successors reversed his policies, the Crusaders made their way to Palestine in order to wrest control of the holy places from the Muslims. They rebuilt many of the

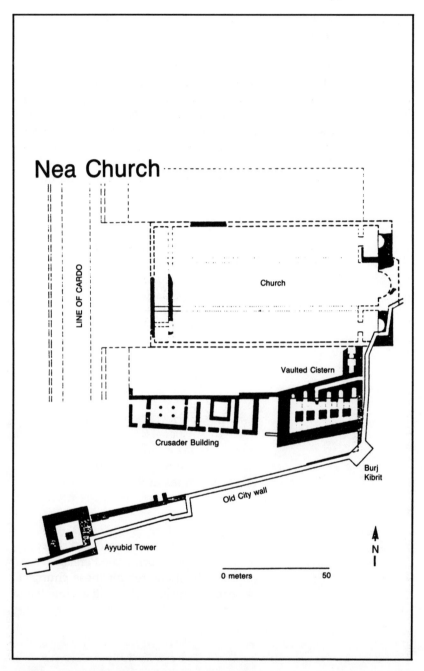

ILLUSTRATION 35. THE NEA CHURCH. This was the "new" church in honor of
Mary built by Justinian.

Byzantine churches. What visitors to Jerusalem today see are not the Byzantine churches but their Crusader successors.

The most significant quality of the building of the Byzantine church commemorating the death and resurrection of Jesus was its location. The site was chosen because of its association in the memory of the indigenous Christian community with the location of Jesus' tomb. Though the Romans under Hadrian tried to obliterate that memory by building a temple to Venus on the site, they were unsuccessful. It is highly probable that the Church of the Holy Sepulchre—the successor of Constantine's basilica—encloses both Calvary and the tomb of Jesus. It is no wonder, then that this church is a powerful magnet drawing pilgrims from around the world.

Chapter 10

The Churches of Central
and Southern Palestine

Introduction

Most of the ancient churches of Palestine were built for the sake of congregational worship. Only a small number were built as memorials to some event in the life of Jesus. The latter tended to be concentrated in Jerusalem and Galilee—in particular around the northwestern shore of the Sea of Galilee. The rest of Galilee had few churches since the Galilee of the Byzatine period was the Jewish stronghold in Palestine. The Christian population of Palestine, and consequently most of the churches, were concentrated in central and southern Palestine. In addition the Judean desert was a magnet for many Christians attracted to the monastic life, and so that area was dotted with monastic settlements with their own churches. There were once more than 130 churches in central and southern Palestine.

This chapter will describe just a few of the many churches found in this region. Of these, three will be memorial churches associated with some event in Jesus' life, and two will be congregational churches built to serve the needs of Christians in Avdat, a town in the Negev region of southern Palestine.

The Church of Jacob's Well

Jacob's well is located in Shechem, the most important city for the Samaritans, since their temple was built on the crest of Mount Gerezim in whose shadow Shechem stands. The Book of Acts describes the early success that the gospel enjoyed among the Samaritans (8:5-25). The Gospels are, however, somewhat ambivalent toward them. Matthew has Jesus forbidding the disciples to enter Samaritan towns (10:5) though both Luke (10:30-37; 17:11-19) and John (4:4-42) portray

Jesus as friendly toward Samaritans. Even when a certain Samaritan village refused to receive him, Jesus did not condemn it but simply moved on to another town, though James and John urged Jesus to send "fire from heaven" to consume the inhospitable villagers (Luke 9:51-56). Toward the end of the fourth century a cruciform church was built at the site of Jacob's well near Shechem to commemorate Jesus' conversation with the Samaritan woman at the well, recounted in John 4:5-42 (see illust. 36). Evidently, the town was an important Christian center even before the Byzantine period. Literary sources indicate that the bishop of "Flavia Neapolis"—as Shechem was known in the Roman period—attended local church councils in 314 and the Ecumenical Council of Nicaea in 325.

Shechem plays an important role in the Jacob traditions (Gen 25:19-35:29). According to Genesis 33:18-20 Jacob finally made his home in Shechem, the principal city of central Canaan. No doubt, once Jacob settled there he had to find his own source of water because water rights to the springs in the area would have been assigned long before. After all, the area had been settled since the Chalcolithic period (4500-3100 B.C.E.). A relative latecomer, Jacob had to dig his own well if he wanted water for his family and flocks. The tradition preserved in John 4:6, which associates the well of Sychar to Jacob, has the ring of probability to it.

The name Sychar is probably a Greek corruption of Shechem. Ancient Shechem was an important city during the Bronze Age, long before the Israelites settled in Canaan. The city was located at the center of an ancient road system. It guarded the only east-west pass in the region and it was surrounded by springs. It was an ideal place for a city. The people of the town made a covenant with the Israelite tribes entering Canaan (Josh 24) and so the city was unaffected by the conflicts that took place during the settlement period. Shechem remained an important Israelite city until the capital of the Northern Kingdom was moved to the newly built Samaria a few kilometers north. Later the city became a Samaritan center because of its proximity to Mount Gerezim and its temple. This temple was destroyed in 128 B.C. by the Jewish king, John Hyrcanus. This act cemented feelings of hostility between Samaritans and Jews forever. In Jesus' day memories of that temple were still vivid (John 4:20). The current name of Shechem is Nablus. This name is an Arabic corruption of the name of a military colony, built by the Romans for the veterans of the First Revolt—Flavia Neapolis. The town remains an important Samaritan center, for many of the descendants of that ancient people live there.

During his seventh-century visit to Shechem, Arculf drew a diagram of a church that he saw in the city. His plan showed a cruciform

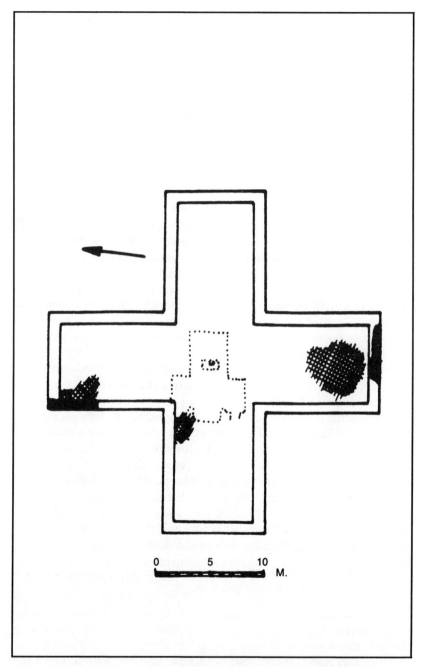

ILLUSTRATION 36. THE CHURCH OVER JACOB'S WELL IN SHECHEM (NABLUS). Note
the cruciform shape of the church with Jacob's Well at the center.

edifice in the center of which was Jacob's well. The church became a famous place of pilgrimage because of its association with the incident involving Jesus and the Samaritan woman who offered Jesus a drink from Jacob's well.[1] The Madaba map which dates from the sixth century, however, shows the church to have been a rectangular building—not a cruciform one. The area has not been subjected to systematic excavation though it has been surveyed, but an accurate description of the structures that stood on this site is not possible.[2] The published plan of the church has been reconstructed on the basis of the architectural elements that are visible at the site together with Arculf's sketch.

According to this sketch, in the center of the cruciform building was Jacob's well. The four arms of the building extend from this center.[3] At the end of each arm was a small church. The overall length of the structure was thirty meters and the width of each arm was nine meters. There was no apse in the church since worship was oriented toward the well in the center. Portions of a mosaic were found near the well. The fragments shows a multicolored geometric pattern. According to a sixth-century description of the church there was a chancel screen around the well and fragments of that screen have been found. The decorations on the fragments were those characteristic of the Byzantine period. A Samaritan inscription was found which probably came from the Byzantine church, though it was reused in the later Crusader church. This inscription contains the Samaritan version of the Ten Commandments.

Dating the church on archaeological grounds is difficult because systematic excavations have not been done. Literary remains indicate that a church existed over Jacob's Well by the end of the fourth century. Whether this is the same church that Arculf saw some three hundred years later is not certain. Only careful excavation will answer some of the questions regarding the Church of Jacob's Well.

The church was destroyed by the Arabs in the tenth century. In 1130 the Crusaders built another church which did not follow the pattern of the earlier church but followed the more typical romanesque

---

[1] Crowfoot 89–90. This site draws Christian pilgrims who are usually surprised to learn that water can still be drawn from the well.

[2] Reports on these surveys can be found in L. H. Vincent, "Puits de Jacob ou de la Samaritaine," *Revue biblique* 65 (1958) 547–67; and Bellarmino Bagatti, "Nuovi Apporti Archeologici sul Pozzo di Giacobbe in Samaria," *Liber Annuus* 16 (1965–66) 127–64.

[3] The only parts of the structure that actually have been identified are a part of the southern wall of the southern arm and a part of the western wall of the northern arm. See Ovadiah and Gomez de Silva 1981, 245.

style of crusader churches. The well was incorporated into the crypt of the Crusader church. The Crusader church was destroyed in 1238. There was an attempt at the beginning of this century to restore it, but the effort was abandoned before reconstruction progressed very far.

The Church of the Theotokos on Mount Gerezim

The indigenous population of Palestine chafed under Roman and Byzantine occupation. There were a number of revolts against the occupying powers. The Christian Byzantines were no less ruthless in putting down these revolts than were the Romans. On Mount Gerezim there is a church dedicated to Mary under her title as the Mother of God. It was built by the Byzantines not only to honor Mary but more so to celebrate their victory over the rebellious Samaritans who revolted against them in 484. Near the top of Mount Gerezim, a place sacred to the Samaritans, the Emperor Zeno built a church which looked down on Jacob's well where Jesus told the Samaritan woman that true worship of God would take place neither in Jerusalem or on Gerezim but in spirit and truth (John 4:21). In fact, Terebinthius, the bishop of Flavia Neapolis when this church was built, saw its construction as the fulfillment of Jesus' words.[4]

The church on Mount Gerezim was first surveyed in the nineteenth century and the first full-scale excavations were directed by G. Welter and A. M. Schneider of the German Institute in 1928. Their excavations revealed that the Theotokos church was meant more as a statement to the Samaritans who lived below in Shechem and who came to pray on Mount Gerezim than it was a monument to Christian piety. The church was an octagon whose interior diameter was 21.40 meters (see illust. 37). The length of each side of the octagon was 8.8 meters. The western arm of the octagon was a narthex with three monumental entrances that opened into the center of the octagon. Opposite the narthex was an apse that had a triumphal arch standing in front of it. The apse was located between the pastophoria though there is no sign of an ambo, altar, or a synthronos, making it quite probable that this church was not intended as a setting for liturgical services. Finally, there were smaller chapels in four of the arms of the octagon. The building was constructed of local stone which was beautifully worked. The interior walls were all faced with polished marble. The floors were covered by mosaics with geometric patterns and some of the walls may have been adorned with mosaics as well. The one Greek inscription

[4] Crowfoot 1941, 92, no. 1.

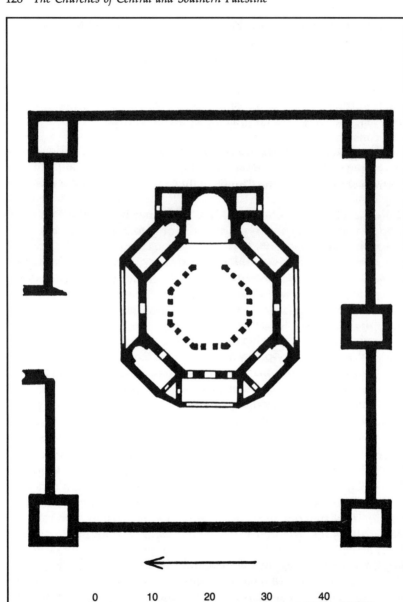

ILLUSTRATION 37. THE CHURCH OF THE THEOTOKOS ON MOUNT GEREZIM. The octagonal church was set within a fortress.

found at the site indicated that a fragment of the rock of Calvary was one of the relics housed in the church.[5]

The church is completely surrounded by a rectangular wall that was protected by five turrets. In spite of these defensive measures, the church was probably damaged during the Samaritan revolt of 532. After putting down that uprising, Justinian rebuilt this shrine in honor of Mary, the Mother of God. The excavation of this church reveals that the construction of a church could be as much a political statement as a religious one. Certainly the Samaritans living in Shechem got a message from the Byzantines each time the Samaritans looked at the fortress which housed the Church of the Theotokos on Mount Gerezim.

Emmaus

The story of the risen Lord's appearance before two disciples on the road to Emmaus (Luke 24:13-35) is one of the best known tales in the New Testament. Naturally, pious Christians would want to memorialize the events of the Lucan narrative, but it was difficult to locate the site of first century Emmaus. Some manuscripts of Luke state that Emmaus was sixty stadia (about seven miles) from Jerusalem; other manuscripts give the distance to be 160 stadia (about nineteen miles). This discrepancy among the ancient manuscripts, and the lack of a pre-Constantinian tradition about the location of Emmaus, has led to four sites being identified with the Emmaus of Jesus' day.

Emmaus is mentioned in accounts of the Maccabean wars (1 Macc 3:40, 57; 4:3) as the location of an important battle between the Jews and the Syrians. The violence that took place there during the second century B.C.E. presaged the tragic history of this town. In 43 B.C.E. the inhabitants of Emmaus were sold into slavery by the Romans for nonpayment of taxes. Three years later the Romans set fire to the town because of the disturbances which broke out there following Herod's death. The Roman Fifth Legion encamped there during the First Revolt. During the Second Revolt, the Roman garrison from Petra was stationed in Emmaus. After all these disruptions it was no wonder that the town was largely abandoned until the third century C.E.

In 221 the city was reconstructed under a charter granted by the Emperor Elagabalus to Julius Africans and renamed Nicopolis ("the city of victory"). Writing in the late fourth century, Jerome notes the name change and asserts that Nicopolis was, in fact, the Emmaus of Luke 24. Jerome is simply reflecting the tradition that was first stated by Eusebius early in the century.[6] During the Byzantine period, an im-

---

[5] Crowfoot 1941, 94.
[6] Murphy-O'Connor 1986, 270–71.

posing triapsidal basilica was built in Nicopolis. In 639 the city was depopulated by a plague that eventually spread throughout the Middle East. It is interesting to note that when the Arabs refer to this city, they do not use the Roman-Byzantine name, Nicopolis, but revert to the old semitic name of Emmaus which they preserve as Imwas.

Because of its strategic location, the Crusaders stationed a garrison near the site of the Byzantine church. They built a church inside the central apse and nave of the Byzantine church by reusing portions of the Byzantine-period ruins. The Crusaders did not memorialize the events of Luke 24 at this site, for they believed Emmaus was located in Abu Gosh which was the site of a village within the sixty-stadia boundary of some manuscripts of Luke. Evidently, they had no idea that Imwas was where Byzantine Christians believed the two disciples were going when they met Jesus. From the beginning of the sixteenth century, Qubeiba—a third site—became associated with Luke 24.[7]

Jerome Murphy-O'Connor argues that neither Imwas, Abu Gosh, nor Qubeiba was the site of ancient Emmaus. He suggests a site much closer to Jerusalem (only thirty stadia). In the first century the suggested village was populated by Roman veterans from the wars of the First Revolt and renamed "Colonia," a name preserved until recently by Qoloniya, the Arabic village on the site.[8]

Because of its strategic location on the road to Jerusalem, the site of the Byzantine Emmaus was the scene of very bitter fighting during the 1948 Arab-Israeli War. The roadside is still littered with the hulks of the armored vehicles that failed to make it to Jerusalem. After the 1967 war Imwas was once again depopulated and the area was turned into a park.

The site of Byzantine Emmaus was excavated by two Dominicans from the École Biblique, L. H. Vincent and F. M. Abel, from 1924 to 1927.[9] They identified five separate structures on the site. The earliest remains were the foundations of walls from the second and first centuries B.C.E. The second structure built on the site was a large Roman villa of the second century C.E. The villa was almost square (eighteen by seventeen meters). Its floors were adorned with mosaics of geometric, floral, and faunal figures. These mosaics were reused in the next building erected on the site: a Christian church. A third structure

---

[7] Qubeiba is the place usually shown to contemporary pilgrims as the site of Emmaus.

[8] Murphy-O'Connor 1986, 271. He maintains that sixty stadia reflects the distance given by Luke but that it should be understood as representing the distance for a round trip between Jerusalem and Emmaus.

[9] They published the report of their excavations in a joint work, *Emmaus, sa basilique et son histoire* (Paris, 1932).

was identified by Vincent and Abel as a third-century Christian triapsidal basilica (46.4 by 24.4 meters), though hardly anyone agrees with
Vincent's dating of the basilica.[10] The interior space of the building was
divided into a nave and two aisles by two rows of thirteen columns
(see illust. 38). North of this building was a separate baptistery (10.5
by 10.5 meters). It was fed by a well just to the north of the building.
In front of the baptistery was another basilica (20 by 10.2 meters) with
a single central apse. A narthex faced the front of the northern basilica. Finally, Vincent and Abel identified a Romanesque Crusader
church from the twelfth century which reused the central apse of the
southern church.

There are no inscriptions or mosaics to indicate that the Byzantines intended to memorialize the events of Luke 24 with these buildings. The identification of this site already in the fourth century by
Eusebius and Jerome as the Emmaus of Luke's Gospel makes it probable that the builders of the fifth-century church believed that their
church stood on the site of first century Emmaus. Perhaps they even
thought that the Roman villa on the ruins of which they erected their
basilica were the remnants of Cleopas' home where Jesus broke bread
with the two disciples.

The Churches of Avdat

The New Testament preserves no tradition of Jesus journeying to
the Negev, the arid region in southern Palestine. In fact, it was not
until the beginning of the second century C.E. that this region was incorporated into the Roman Empire. From at least the fourth century
B.C.E. this region was controlled by the Nabateans, an Arab tribe whose
headquarters were in Petra. Important trade routes passed through
the Negev and the Nabateans derived a significant amount of wealth
from the regulation of trade in the region. They were so powerful that
the Roman government did not even try to oppose them until the second century when changed economic conditions put an end to Nabatean dominance in the Negev. Eventually the Nabateans assimilated
into other elements of the local population and disappeared from the
pages of history.

[10] Most people reject Vincent's date on historical grounds. In the third century Christianity was both a prohibited and a persecuted religion. The building
of such an impressive structure would have been out of the question. Also, the
triapsidal form did not become popular until the fifth century. See Ovadiah 1970,
64. What makes firm dating almost impossible is the failure of the excavators to
record any ceramic findings associated with the various phases of occupation at
the site.

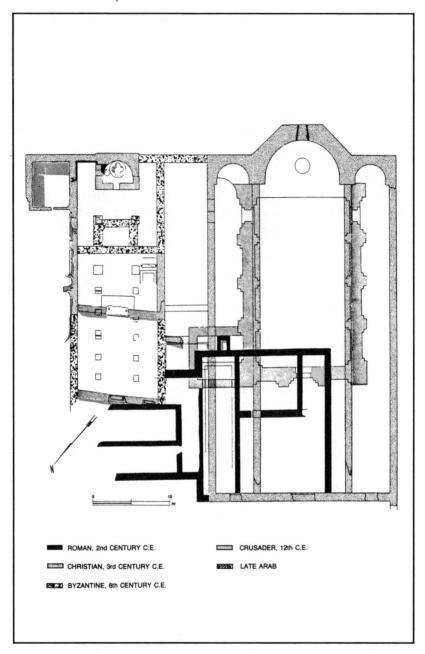

ILLUSTRATION 38. THE CHURCH (right) AND BAPTISTERY (left) AT IMWAS (THE BYZANTINE EMMAUS). The structure to the left of the baptistery was a cistern that fed the baptismal font.

Once the regulation of trade was no longer lucrative, the people of the Negev turned to agriculture. To be successful the people had to overcome the inhospitable conditions of the desert. They adopted techniques developed first by the Nabateans to make the most of the little rain that falls in the desert (only about one hundred millimeters annually). They succeeded, and many Nabatean cities experienced a revival during the late Roman and Byzantine periods. Avdat was one of the Nabatean cities which enjoyed an influx of new inhabitants at this time. Its population increased to about three thousand. Most of these immigrants engaged in agricultural pursuits. Avdat became rather famous as a center for the production of grapes and wine.[11]

To protect the people of Avdat the Byzantine authorities built a fortress on the acropolis of the city.[12] Within that fortress there were three Christian churches (see illust. 39). The oldest of these was called simply "the north church," and is dated to the fifth century. The church was a basilica with a single apse. The church was not oriented toward true east because of the constraints resulting from its location on Avdat's acropolis. The single apse was not aligned directly with the nave in an attempt to correct the slightly skewed orientation of the building. There was an atrium directly in front of the church and in the atrium's center was a cistern. There was a triple entrance way into the church (20 by 14.40 meters) that had two rows of five columns. There was a small baptistery in a portico just west of the church. It had separate fonts for adults and children. The sanctuary area or bema was raised about two steps above the nave and was separated from it by a chancel screen that was about three feet high. Just outside the screen was the ambo or pulpit. Within the apse was as episcopal throne and the foundation of the synthronos for the rest of the clergy. The pastophoria were on either side of the apse. The floor of the church was stone slabs.

When the south wall of the church was dismantled, it was evident that the Byzantine church was built of materials from the temple to

[11] Contemporary agricultural experts are studying the ancient methods of desert farming first developed by the Nabateans in view of applying them today. The region around Avdat is still famous for its wine. One of the popular brands of wine in Israel carried the Avdat label.

[12] Though the ruins of Avdat were surveyed by A. Musil, C. L. Wooley, and T. E. Lawrence at the beginning of the twentieth century, they were systematically excavated for the first time by M. Avi-Yonah and A. Negev between 1958 and 1961. Their work was sponsored by the Israeli Department of Antiquities, the Hebrew University, and the Israel Exploration Society. For a bibliography of reports on these excavations see Ovadiah 1970, 26, Vogel 1971, 3, and Vogel and Holtzclaw 1982, 3.

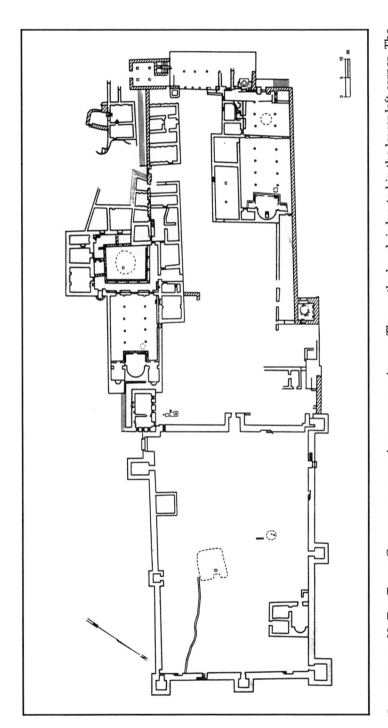

ILLUSTRATION 39. THE THREE CHURCHES ON THE ACROPOLIS OF AVDAT. The north church is located in the lower left corner. The south church (Saint Theodore) is toward the center and left. The small chapel within the fortress is the apsidal structure set in the north wall.

Zeus (Roman period) which stood in the same area. The builders of the Byzantine church turned the stone moldings of this pagan temple in such a way that none of their motifs would be visible to the Christian worshipper. The church was destroyed by fire during the Persian invasion in the early seventh century and was never rebuilt. Pillars and capitals from the church were found in the cistern located in the atrium. They were placed there when the structure was cleared by Arabs who turned the church into a pen for sheep.

The second church on Avdat's acropolis was part of a monastic complex. Excavators believe the rooms surrounding the church were cells for the monks. In addition, five tombs were discovered in the aisles of the church, one in the prothesis and three in the atrium.[13] An inscription on one of the tombs mentions a monastery. According to another tomb inscription the church was dedicated to Saint Theodore. Another inscription dates the church to 541.

Like the north church this church is also slightly askew. It could not be oriented directly toward the east because it abutted a preexisting Roman tower. In front of the monastic church was an atrium with a peristyle. In the center of the atrium was a cistern. The south church measured 21 by 12.60 meters and had a triple apse instead of a single one like the north church. It was a basilica with two rows of five columns. Its chancel had an unusual T-shape with a bema raised two steps above the nave. Portions of an altar were found as was the foundation for the ambo. The central entrance in the western wall was the most splendid of the three doorways into the church. The capitals of its door posts were Nabatean. Apparently, the Byzantine architects simply reused a monumental entranceway to one of the old Nabatean buildings of Avdat. The rest of the building materials were hewn and dressed by the builders of this church. Finally, some of the rooms alongside the church were decorated with wall paintings depicting various saints.

A third church was found on the acropolis. It was a small chapel probably erected in the sixth century at the same time the fortress was built on the east end of the acropolis. Its design was quite simple. Since it was built adjoining the north wall of the fortress, its constructors had to build only three more walls. It had but one entrance from the west and a single apse. It was built probably to serve the religious needs of soldiers who defended Avdat.

[13] Burial in Palestinian churches is quite rare and is usually restricted to members of the clergy. At least three of the people buried in the south church at Avdat were laypeople. Burials of laity in churches seems to have been restricted to the churches of the Negev. See A. Negev, "The Churches of the Central Negev An Archaeological Survey," *Revue Biblique* (1974) 407.

There were at least fifteen other churches in the Negev. All of them served local congregations since the Negev was not a center for pilgrimage. Some of these churches were part of monastic settlements but most were built during the Byzantine period when the empire tried to exploit the meager agricultural resources of the arid region.

Excursus: The Madaba Map

In 1884, while laying the foundations for a new Greek Orthodox church in a Transjordanian village called Madaba (Hebrew: *Medeba*), a group of workmen came upon a mosaic from a sixth-century Byzantine church that was, in fact, the oldest surviving map of Palestine. The discovery was duly noted in the church's archives but authorities were unaware of the mosaic's significance, and construction on the new church went ahead, causing considerable damage to the mosaic. Some twelve years later the librarian of the Greek Orthodox Patriarchate visited Madaba and immediately recognized the significance of the mosaic. He made the scholarly world aware of its existence, and since then interest in Madaba and its map has remained constant.

In the thirteenth century B.C.E., Madaba was a Moabite town. Control of the town passed back and forth between Israel and Moab until the Hasmonean period, when John Hyrcanus II handed the town over to the Nabateans.[14] It remained under Nabatean rule until the beginning of the second century C.E. when the Nabatean Kingdom was incorporated into the Roman Province of Arabia. The Mishnah testifies to a Jewish presence in the city as late as the second century C.E.[15] The presence of Madaba's bishop at the Council of Chalcedon fifth century attests to Christian presence in the town. In the Byzantine period there were at least ten churches in the city. One of these churches contained the famous mosaic.

Though the mosaic did not survive intact, it is apparent that it depicted the entire biblical world with Jerusalem at its center.[16] The

[14] Biblical references to Madaba include Numbers 21:30; Joshua 13:9, 16; 2 Samuel 10:1; 1 Chronicles 19:7. Josephus records the Hasmonean capture of the city (*Antiquities* 13:255) and the gift of the town by John Hyrcanus II to the Nabateans (*Antiquities,* 13:18).

[15] *Mikva'ot* 7:1.

[16] For more complete descriptions of the map see Victor R. Gold, "The Mosaic Map of Madeba," *Biblical Archeologist* 21 (1958) 50–71, reprinted in *Biblical Archeologist Reader 3*, eds. E. F. Campbell and D. N. Freedman (Garden City, N.Y.: Doubleday, 1970) 366–89; Michael Avi-Yonah and Ephraim Stern, *Encyclopedia of Archeological Excavations in the Holy Land* (Englewood Cliff, N.J.: Prentice-Hall, 1977) 3:819-23. A more complete bibliography in Madaba and its mosaic can be found in Vogel 1971, 57; and Vogel and Holtzclaw 1982, 54.

scale of the map is generally 1:15,000, though important sites such as Jerusalem are depicted out of scale. Like all ancient maps of the region, its point of orientation is eastward. The map depicts settlements, important structures, and topographic details of Palestine. Large cities, such as Jerusalem and Neapolis (Nablus-Shechem), are presented in some detail with their public buildings—and in particular their churches—being highlighted.

The importance of the map has little to do with the identification of Palestine's natural features, nor even its identification of biblical sites. The former have not changed significantly since the sixth century, and the latter can be identified by using Eusebius' *Onomasticon*. In fact, the map takes two-thirds of its identifications from Eusebius. Most of these identifications, however, are not acceptable to scholars today. The map's primary value is its faithful visual rendering of the way Palestine looked in the Byzantine period. Its depiction of some churches helps to determine how these buildings looked, given that little of the original buildings has survived. The mosaic is composed of about 2.5 million tesserae and probably took more than a year to lay. The mosaic testifies to the interest people of the Byzantine period had in the history of Palestine, and their determination to provide a record of their own accomplishments for future generations.

Conclusion

The archaeological findings presented throughout this study demonstrate the ways in which archaeology itself has broadened our understanding and appreciation of the formative years of both Judaism and Christianity. I hope the reader will conclude that the archaeological study of Palestine's early synagogues and churches should not be relegated to the history of art and architecture, but should become part of any attempt to understand the religious faith and practices of early Judaism and Christianity. Scientific examination of these ancient structures is important, not simply as a way of learning how architectural forms developed over the years, but also as a way of perceiving how religious faith expressed itself beyond its sacred texts. This is especially important today when an understanding of the social setting of early Judaism and Christianity has been recognized as vital by contemporary scholarship. How can that social setting be faithfully recreated without familiarity with the findings of archaeology?

This book has also described some outstanding problems related to ancient synagogues and churches that still need resolution. Three principal questions about *synagogues* still have not received completely satisfactory answers. First, when and where did the synagogue as a religious institution originate, and when were the first synagogues built? Second, how is a building recognized as a synagogue? Finally, to what extent will the controversial dating of the Capernaum synagogue stimulate a rethinking of previously held conclusions about Galilean synagogues and about relation between Jews and Christians? An important problem raised by the excavation of Christian churches concerns Jewish Christianity: How can this phenomenon be described? How long did it last? What structures can be identified as Jewish Christian synagogues or churches?

This has not been a systematic study of Jewish and Christian architecture in Palestine during the Roman and Byzantine periods. The state of scholarship in this area of archaeology does not allow such a systematic presentation. The kind of interpretive work that integrates information from literary and archaeological sources is just beginning.

Archaeologists are starting to broaden their horizons beyond simple description to include the interpretation of data. Conversely, interpreters of the literary traditions are beginning to realize how necessary it is to consider the findings archaeology has brought to light. In the future the most academically valuable studies of Judaism and Christianity's formative years will be those that integrate literary and archaeological scholarship.

This study has also presented some positive conclusions about both early Judaism and Christianity. First, it has shown that both traditions have been willing and able to take an "alien" architectural form and adapt it for their own use. Both, for example, take the Greco-Roman basilica and make it serve their own distinctive liturgical needs. This demonstrates both a degree of accommodation to hellenistic culture and a fidelity to religious tradition. The practice of accommodation is especially interesting. Some Jewish communities kept decoration in the synagogue to a minimum while others included not only geometric and floral designs but also portraits of human beings and even pagan deities. Apparently, not all Jews interpreted in precisely the same way the commandment forbidding the making of images. Their religious architecture and art were influenced as much by current fashions and popular beliefs as by "orthodox" religious tenets. The ability of Christian architects to be innovative within their cultural setting is evident in the development of the transept, which effectively expressed the centrality of the cross in Christian faith.

The variety of architectural forms and variations discovered shows there was no such thing as a typical church or synagogue. Any portrayal of early Judaism or Christianity as monochromatic is disproven by a survey of the settings in which Jews or Christians chose to worship. Some structures were very simple while others were quite ornate. At times, the extravagance of certain building projects was not so much an expression of the local piety as it was a sign of the economic prosperity of particular donors, whether they were local people or imperial benefactors.

This book has introduced the reader to some issues and problems that need to be faced when one wishes to understand how the Jews and Christians of the Roman and Byzantine periods understood, defined, and expressed themselves through their religious architecture. The guiding assumption throughout this work has been that these people are worth knowing. After all, Jews and Christians today understand and define themselves, in part, within categories first developed by these people—our predecessors in the faith.

Sources of the Illustrations

1. Map of Ancient Synagogue Sites in Palestine reprinted with permission of Carta, Jerusalem, Israel.

2. Lee I. Levine, *Ancient Synagogues Revealed,* Israel Exploration Society, Jerusalem, Israel.

3. Eric M. Meyers and James F. Strange, *Archaeology, the Rabbis and Early Christianity* (Nashville: Abingdon, 1981). fig. 12.

4. Levine, *Ancient Synagogues Revealed.*

5. Michael Avi-Yonah and Ephraim Stern, *Encyclopedia of Archaeological Excavations in the Holy Land [EAEHL],* (Giratayim, Israel: Massada Press, 1977) 4:1096.

6. *New Encyclopedia of Archaeological Excavations in the Holy Land,* Israel Exploration Society, Jerusalem, Israel.

7. Ibid.

8. Levine, *Ancient Synagogues Revealed.*

9. Ibid.

10. Ibid.

11. Ibid.

12. Ibid.

13. Rachel P.L. H. Vincent, ''Un sanctuaire dans la region de Jericho la synagogue de Naʿaran, *Revue biblique* 68:163–77.

14. Richard Krautheimer, *Early Christian and Byzantine Architecture* (London: Penguin Books, 1975) 61.

15. *Schweich Lectures on Biblical Archaeology, 1937, Early Churches in Palestine* (London: The British Academy) by J. W. Crowfoot, p. 78, fig. 16.

16. *EAEHL* 3:919.

17. B. Bagatti, *Excavations in Nazareth* (Jerusalem: Franciscan Printing Press, 1969) 1:154.

18–20. Meyers and Strange, *Archaeology, the Rabbis and Early Christianity,* figs. 4, 5, 6.

21. Photographic Archive, Archaeological Expedition at Capernaum/Emmanuele Testa. Biblical Archaeology Society, Washington, D.C.

22. John Wilkinson, *Egeria's Travels* (London: SPCK, 1971) 195.

23. Ibid., 197.

24. Ibid., 198.

25. Bernhard Gauer © 1932. Biblical Archaeology Society, Washington, D.C.

26. Bargil Pixner, "The Miracle Church of Tabgha on the Sea of Galilee," *Biblical Archaeologist* 48/4 (December 1985) 201.

27. Wilkinson, *Egeria's Travels*, 199.

28. Asher Ovadiah, "Supplementum to the Corpus of Byzantine Churches" *Levant* 13 (University of Edinburgh: The British School of Archaeology in Jerusalem, 1981) 239.

29. *EAEHL*, 1:304.

30. Asher Ovadiah, *Corpus of the Byzantine Churches in the Holy Land* (Bonn: Peter Hanstein Verlag, 1970) pl. 30, no. 65a.

31. Ibid., pl. 30, no. 65b.

32. Ibid., pl. 33, no. 71.

33. Ibid., pl. 36, no. 74a.

34. John Flower, *Jerusalem* (The Blue Guide, Huntington, England: A & C Black, 1989) 262.

35. Ibid., 230.

36. Ovadiah, "Supplementum," 245.

37. Ovadiah, *Corpus*, pl. 57, no. 143.

38. *EAEHL*, 2:364.

39. *EAEHL*, 2:348.

The Liturgical Press gratefully thanks the publishers of the above titles for granting permission to reprint the illustrations.

Glossary

aedicula (pl: *aediculae*): Literally "little building;" a small structure which generally housed the Torah scrolls of a synagogue.

apse: The rounded end of a synagogue or church which served as the focus of worship.

ashlar: A large paving stone

basilica: A rectangular hall whose interior space is divided by two rows of columns.

bema: A low dais found in churches and synagogues. It served to raise the space that was the focus of worship above that occupied by the congregation.

broadhouse: A rectangular building whose wall or orientation is one of the long walls.

Byzantine Period: That part of Palestine's history which extends approximately three hundred years from the time of Constantine (313) until the Arab conquest (640).

casemate wall: A hollow wall. During peace time, the rooms in the wall could be used for various purposes. During war, these rooms would be filled with stone and debris to strengthen the wall in case of siege.

diaconicon: The robing room for the clergy in Byzantine churches

ethrog: A cirtron; a citrus fruit used during the rituals connected with the Feast of Booths (Sukkoth).

horvah(t): Hebrew for ruin.

khirbeh(t): Arabic for ruin.

lulab: The palm branch used during the rituals of Sukkoth.

menorah (pl: *menoroth*): The lamp stand of the Temple. Copies of the Temple's lamp stand were found frequently in synagogues.

Mishnah: The earliest codification of Jewish oral law (200 C.E.) by Judah the Prince.

narthex: A portico which stood in front of churches separating the sacred space of the church from the profane world.

ostracon: A fragment of pottery bearing an inscription.

pastophoria: The sacristy of Byzantine churches. It consisted of two rooms usually found on either side of the central apse: the *prothesis* and the *diaconicon.*

pediment: The triangular gabled end of a roof in Greco-Roman buildings.

peristyle: A row of columns surrounding an atrium.

prothesis: A room in Byzantine churches employed to prepare the offerings used in the liturgy.

Roman Period: That part of Palestine's history which began with Pompey's conquest (63 B.C.E.) and continued to the rule of Constantine (313 C.E.).

shofar: A ram's horn trumpet.

stylobate: A support for a row of columns.

Talmud: The corpus of rabbinic civil and ceremonial law. It exists in two editions—one coming from Palestine (fifth century C.E.) and the other from Babylon (seventh century C.E.).

tessera (pl: *tesserae*): The individual pieces that form a mosaic.

transept: That part of a cruciform church that crosses at right angles to the nave.

triclinium: A formal dining area. Its furnishings consist of a table and three surrounding couches, from which the dining room takes its name in latinized Greek.

Bibliography

Avi-Yonah, Michael, and Ephraim Stern. *Encyclopedia of Archaeological Excavations in the Holy Land.* 4 vols. Englewood Cliffs, N.J.: Prentice-Hall, 1977.

Bagatti, Bellarmino, O.F.M. *The Church from the Circumcision.* Jerusalem: Franciscan Printing Press, 1971.

Chiat, Marilyn Joyce Segal. *Handbook of Synagogue Architecture.* Brown Judaic Studies 29. Chico, Calif.: Scholars Press, 1982.

Crowfoot, J. W. *Early Churches in Palestine.* London: The British Academy, 1941.

Gutmann, Joseph, ed. *Ancient Synagogues.* Brown Judaic Studies 22. Chico, Calif.: Scholars Press, 1981.

_____. *The Synagogue.* The Library of Biblical Studies. New York: Ktav, 1975.

Hoppe, Leslie J. *What Are They Saying about Biblical Archaeology?* New York: Paulist, 1984.

Krautheimer, Richard. *Early Christian and Byzantine Architecture.* Revised edition. Baltimore: Penguin Books, 1975.

Levine, Lee I., ed. *Ancient Synagogues Revealed.* Detroit: Wayne State University Press, 1982.

_____. *The Synagogue in Late Antiquity.* Philadelphia: The American Schools of Oriental Research, 1987.

Meyers, Eric M., and James F. Strange. *Archaeology, the Rabbis and Early Christianity.* Nashville: Abingdon, 1981.

Migne, J. P. *Patrologiae cursus completus. Series graeca.* Paris: J. P. Migne, 1863.

Murphy-O'Connor, Jerome. *The Holy Land: An Archaeological Guide from the Earliest Times to 1700.* Second edition. Oxford: Oxford University Press, 1986.

Ovadiah, Asher. *Corpus of the Byzantine Churches in the Holy Land.* Bonn: Peter Hanstein Verlag, 1970.

_____. and Carla Gomez de Silva. "Supplementum to the Corpus of the Byzantine Churches in the Holy Land." *Levant* 13 (1981) 200–261; 14 (1982), 122–70; 16 (1984), 129–65.

Sukenik, E. L. *Ancient Synagogues in Palestine and Greece.* London: Oxford University Press, 1934.

Vogel, Eleanor K. *Bibliography of Holy Land Sites.* Part I. Cincinnati: Hebrew Union College-Jewish Institute of Religion, 1971.

Vogel, Eleanor K. and Brooks Holtzclaw. *Bibliography of Holy Land Sites.* Part II (1970–81). Cincinnati: Hebrew Union College-Jewish Institute of Religion, 1982.

Wigoder, Geoffrey. *The Story of the Synagogue.* San Francisco: Harper & Row, 1986.
Wilkinson, John. *Egeria's Travels.* London: SPCK, 1971.